A FIELD GUIDE TO
THE BUTTERFLIES OF
AFRICA

by John G. Williams

A Field Guide to the Birds of East and Central Africa
A Field Guide to the National Parks of East Africa
A Field Guide to the Butterflies of Africa

The Peterson Identification System
The system of identification in this Field Guide is based on the
original system devised by Roger Tory Peterson.

A FIELD GUIDE TO
THE BUTTERFLIES OF
AFRICA

JOHN G. WILLIAMS

with 24 color plates by the author

HOUGHTON MIFFLIN COMPANY BOSTON
1971

TO DAPHNE

a present-day Aurelian

First American Edition 1971

Copyright © 1969 by John G. Williams

Library of Congress Catalog Card Number: 76-120836

Printed in Great Britain

CONTENTS

Preface		9
Introduction		11
Collecting Butterflies in Africa		20
Papilionidae	Swallowtails	33
Pieridae	Whites	72
Danaidae	Monarchs	100
Acraeidae	Acraeas	106
Nymphalidae	Nymphalids	123
Satyridae	Browns	199
Libytheidae	Snouts	202
Riodinidae	Judys	203
Lycaenidae	Blues	204
Hesperiidae	Skippers	224
Bibliography		227
Index		229

02941

ILLUSTRATIONS

1	Papilionidae – Swallowtails	*facing page* 36
2	Papilionidae – Swallowtails	37
3	Papilionidae – Swallowtails	44
4	Papilionidae – Swallowtails	45
5	Papilionidae – Swallowtails	64
6	Pieridae – Whites	65
7	Pieridae – Whites	80
8	Pieridae – Whites	81
9	Acraeidae and Danaidae – Acraeas and Monarchs	96
10	Nymphalidae	97
11	Nymphalidae	112
12	Nymphalidae	113
13	Nymphalidae	128
14	Nymphalidae	129
15	Nymphalidae	144
16	Nymphalidae	145
17	Nymphalidae	160
18	Nymphalidae	161
19	Nymphalidae	176
20	Nymphalidae	177
21	Nymphalidae	192
22	Nymphalidae	193
23	Libytheidae, Riodinidae and Lycaenidae – Snouts, Judys and Blues	208
24	Lycaenidae – Blues	209

PREFACE

A Field Guide to the Butterflies of Africa has been written expressly for the amateur butterfly collector and for the visitor to Africa who wishes to be able to name the commoner and more colourful butterflies.

In the region covered, Africa south of the Sahara but excluding Madagascar, over 2400 different species of butterflies are known and new species continue to be discovered every year. It is obviously impossible in a book of this scope and size to enumerate and figure all of these. My choice of which butterflies to include has been determined by which families and species are normally represented in collections made by amateur butterfly enthusiasts, together with those which are large and striking in appearance and those which have a wide range throughout most of the Ethiopian Region. Thus, in groups such as the Swallowtails and Charaxes most of the known species are described in detail. Less colourful families such as the Skippers and Browns, of limited appeal to the beginner, necessarily receive much less attention. For the more serious student references to publications on these less popular families are given in a bibliography.

A well-formed collection of butterflies possesses both educational value and aesthetic appeal. However, it cannot be too strongly stressed that the forming of such a collection entails a moral obligation. Butterflies are living creatures of great beauty, not inanimate objects like postage stamps, and it is inexcusable to amass large series of specimens just for personal gratification. The following code of principles should be adopted by anyone who contemplates collecting:

1 To collect in moderation, taking only a few perfect specimens of each species, releasing all those you do not need and those which are damaged.
2 To ensure that all specimens are properly mounted on steel entomological pins.
3 To label every specimen. The data label, a small thin card which is pinned below the butterfly, has a record of the locality in which the specimen was captured, the altitude, date, and name of collector.
4 To ensure that specimens are adequately housed in entomological store-boxes or, better still, cabinet drawers, and that they receive care and attention. To guard against damage by insect pests store-boxes and cabinet drawers must contain naphthalene, which should be replaced at intervals when it evaporates.

5 To consider the collection as being in the nature of a public trust. Provision should be made that it ultimately be presented to a permanent museum or other scientific body. Many collections, sometimes containing rare and scientifically valuable specimens, have in the past been lost by neglect.

It should be the aim of every amateur lepidopterist to try to add to scientific knowledge. It may be that you live in some part of Africa which is imperfectly known so far as its butterfly fauna is concerned. But wherever you are, useful knowledge may be achieved by rearing butterflies from the egg, recording descriptions of the early stages and preserving specimens of these. The eggs, larvae and pupae of many African butterflies, even some of the common ones, are still unknown. Butterfly breeding is a pastime in which the effort expended has a generous recompense. Not only do you obtain perfect specimens for your collection, but you can also have the satisfaction of releasing those you do not need to swell the local population.

There can be few hobbies so absorbing and rewarding as butterfly collecting in Africa. Its pursuance will take you to many wild and beautiful places, and you will gather a harvest of memories of notable captures and discoveries.

ACKNOWLEDGEMENTS

I would wish to record my gratitude to Sir Charles F. Belcher who first introduced me to the beauty of African butterflies, and for the guidance in their study I later received from former colleagues Elliot Pinhey, Robert Carcasson and the late Norman Mitton. I am also most grateful to Mr Ivan Bampton who provided many of the specimens from which I painted the colour plates and made the line drawings, and to my friend Mrs John Ball on whom fell the onerous task of deciphering my handwriting, preparing the typescript and assisting with proof-reading. It is also my pleasure to record my appreciation of the help given to me in the field by many other persons, too numerous to mention individually, and for the unfailing courtesy and sound advice I have always received from my Publishers.

John G. Williams
P.O. Box 729
Nairobi, Kenya
4 April 1968

INTRODUCTION

Recognition of a Butterfly

Butterflies and Moths belong to that vast assemblage of insects known as the Order Lepidoptera, characterised by having the wings covered with minute flat scales, and having in most species a coiled proboscis through which the insect sucks up nourishment.

Within this Order, the natural subdivision is into two sub-orders, Homoneura and Heteroneura. The former is a small primitive group in which the structure of the fore and hindwings is almost identical and there is no coiled proboscis. In the latter – to which the butterflies and most of the moths belong – the structure of the fore and hindwings is dissimilar and there is a coiled proboscis (degenerate in a small number of moths).

The sub-order Heteroneura is divided into eight super-families, one of which, the Papilionoidea, contains all the butterflies including the skippers, although the latter are sometimes accorded the rank of a super-family in their own right. The usual division into 'butterflies' and 'moths', referred to respectively as Rhopalocera and Heterocera, is convenient to use: but it is not a natural classification based on structure and consequently the differences between 'butterflies' and 'moths' are not always clearly defined. However, in the main, butterflies may be recognised on the following characters:

1 Butterflies have a humeral lobe on the hindwings, which takes the place of a coupling apparatus known as the frenulum which is present in most moths and unites the fore and hindwings during flight.

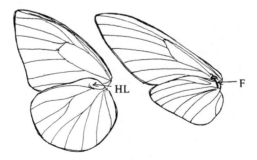

Wings of butterfly and moth, showing humeral lobe (HL) *and frenulum* (F)

2 The antennae of butterflies are thickened or clubbed at the tips (*see figure below*) although in the skippers the antennal clubs are tapered. There is one exception to this rule. This is the remarkable forest-haunting white,

Antennae of butterflies (left) and moths (right)

Pseudopontia paradoxa, whose antennae are thin and attenuated. In moths the structure of the antennae varies greatly in the different families, and may be slender and thread-like, feathery, or gradually thickened. The few moths possessing clubbed antennae may be distinguished from butterflies by the presence of a frenulum.

3 The vast majority of butterflies are diurnal, flying during sunny periods. Exceptions are a few skippers and browns, which are at least partly crepuscular in their appearance. Moths, with some exceptions, are mainly nocturnal.

4 Most butterflies when resting hold their wings together above the body; some skippers are an exception, holding the wings flat. Moths usually rest with their wings folded horizontally over the back so that the upper surface of the forewings is exposed. the hindwings hidden.

Life Cycle of a Butterfly

Butterflies, from egg to adult insect, pass through four distinct stages which are termed the metamorphoses. These are egg (ovum), caterpillar (larva), chrysalis (pupa), and adult insect (imago).

Shortly after mating the female butterfly commences to lay her eggs, usually one or two at a time, on leaves or twigs of the larval food plant. In many species

Butterfly eggs, greatly enlarged

egg-laying continues for a week to ten days or more, the eggs from a single parent being scattered widely thereby ensuring the survival of at least some of the brood.

Eggs vary in structure, being spherical, bottle-shaped or disc-like, often delicately sculptured or ridged. In colour they are usually whitish, yellowish or green.

The eggs hatch after a varying period, not less than seven or eight days, when the young larva eats its way out of the eggshell. It is approximately cylindrical in shape and divided into fourteen segments. The first of these is the head with two groups of simple eyes on each side, a pair of strong jaws and silk-producing organs. Segments two, three and four represent the thorax of the perfect insect and each bears a pair of true legs. Segments five to fourteen correspond to the abdomen of the adult butterfly. Segments seven to ten each possess a pair of fleshy, unjointed 'false legs', and a similar pair on the last segment are called the 'claspers'. All the false legs are lost in the perfect insect.

As the larva grows it changes in both size and form, and the full grown caterpillar may differ greatly from its first appearance. To achieve this the creature's skin is moulted, usually four times during the larval period. The stages between moults are known as instars, and the process of moulting is termed ecdysis.

Larvae of different butterfly families, and even of different genera, vary greatly in structure and appendages. Some examples of these are illustrated.

Larva of Charaxes and Papilio

When the larva is full-grown it often wanders away from the larval food-plant to find a suitable place for pupation. It then spins a silken pad to which it attaches itself by the claspers. In some families, for example the swallow-tails and the whites, it also supports its body with a silken girdle. After resting it moults the skin and emerges as a pupa, the discarded skin being worked backwards to form a wrinkled mass around the tail. The pupa draws its abdomen out of the old skin and attaches itself to the silken pad by means of minute hooks at the tip of the abdomen. Some blues do not attach themselves to a silken pad but pupate on the ground amongst leaves. Skippers usually pupate in a loose cocoon in grass.

When first emerged the pupa is soft and whitish and still capable of considerable movement. Later it contracts somewhat, hardens and becomes completely immobile. As with the larvae, butterfly pupae vary greatly in shape and colour in the different families: some typical examples are illustrated.

Pupa of Papilio and Charaxes

The butterfly remains in the pupal stage for greatly varying periods, sometimes for over a year, although the more usual time is a few weeks.

When the perfect insect is ready to emerge the pupa case splits behind the head. The insect crawls out to rest upside down, often on or near the empty pupa case. The wings at this stage are soft and flabby and only a fraction of their ultimate dimensions. Fluid pumped from the body expands them slowly to their full size. While they are still limp the insect continues to hang upside down, the wings held apart until dry. In small species this drying period takes less than an hour, but in larger species, such as the Charaxes, it may take several hours. The butterfly is then ready to take its first flight. The normal life-span of the perfect butterfly is between two and six weeks.

Identification of African Butterflies

Ten families of butterflies occur on the African continent. These are the Swallowtails (*Papilionidae*), Whites (*Pieridae*), Monarchs or Milkweed Butterflies (*Danaidae*), Browns (*Satyridae*), Nymphalids (*Nymphalidae*), Acraeas (*Acraeidae*), Snouts (*Libytheidae*), Judys (*Riodinidae*), Blues and Coppers (*Lycaenidae*) and Skippers (*Hesperiidae*).

The main characters on which the adult butterflies of these families may be identified are as follows:

SWALLOWTAILS (*Papilionidae*)
Large colourful butterflies, many of which are tailed; all six legs fully developed in both sexes; discoidal cell closed in both fore and hindwings; inner (anal) margin of hindwing without curved abdominal groove, but in males of some species (e.g. *Graphium*) anal margin folded over and containing scent scales or hairs.

Swallowtail

WHITES (*Pieridae*)
Medium-sized butterflies, predominantly white or yellow, often with coloured apical patches; all six legs fully developed in both sexes; inner (anal) margin of hindwing with abdominal groove, but not folded over as in some Papilios; two anal veins on hindwing.

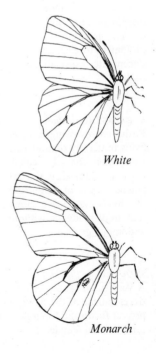

White

MONARCHS (*Danaidae*)
Large conspicuously coloured butterflies, orange-brown, black and white predominating; flight slow and buoyant; cells of both fore and hindwings closed; sac-like pouches of scent scales present on hindwing of male; forelegs of both sexes degenerate and small.

Monarch

BROWNS (*Satyridae*)

Medium-sized mainly brown or grey-ish butterflies, often with eye-spot markings; flight jerky, usually near the ground; cells of both wings closed; veins of forewing much thickened at base; forelegs small and degenerate, covered with hairs; band of scent scales often present on forewing of male.

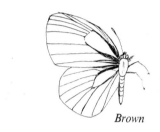

Brown

NYMPHALIDS (*Nymphalidae*)

A large family of mainly robust and colourful butter-flies, many of large size; cell of hindwing open (rarely partially closed by a very fine transverse vein); inner (anal) margin of hindwing with a curved groove to enclose abdomen; forelegs small and degenerate, especially so in male.

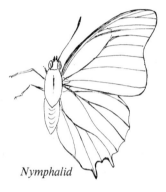

Nymphalid

ACRAEAS (*Acraeidae*)

Rather narrow-winged, slow-flying butterflies of moderate size; often sparsely scaled, with semi-transparent patches; cells of both fore and hindwings closed; inner margin of hindwing without abdominal groove.

Acraea

SNOUTS (*Libytheidae*)

A very small family of medium-sized brown butterflies remarkable for the development of the palpi, which are four times the length of the head and project forwards; forelegs small and degenerate in male, well-developed and functional in female. (*Left*)

Snout

Judy

Blue

JUDYS (*Riodinidae*)
The very few species of this family which occur in Africa are small butterflies with hindwing lobes sharply angled and elongated; forelegs of male small and degenerate, but in female all six legs well-developed and functional. (*Centre*)

BLUES and COPPERS (*Lycaenidae*)
A very large family of small or very small butterflies; many brilliantly coloured, blues predominating, but some coppery-red; many species with long tails; all six legs well-developed and functional in both sexes; antennae placed closely together. (*Right*)

SKIPPERS (*Hesperiidae*)
Small, predominantly dull-coloured butterflies of erratic, rapid flight; body thickset and head wider than thorax; all six legs fully developed and functional in both sexes; antennae with tapered clubs; wing venation distinctive, the veins arising direct from the cell and not branching subsequently.

Skipper

Colour Variation and Mimicry

Many species of butterflies are constant in their general appearance, exhibiting only minor variations of colour, pattern and size. Others, however, exhibit very considerable variation, in extreme cases specimens of the same species being widely dissimilar. Among the latter are those in which the male and female are strikingly different, a variation known as sexual dimorphism; in others there may be more than one type of female, sexual polymorphism. Examples of these are the Diadem (*Hypolimnas misippus*) and the Mocker

Swallowtail (*Papilio dardanus*). Certain butterflies may also differ greatly in their wet season and dry season forms, a phenomenon termed seasonal dimorphism. Striking instances of seasonal dimorphism are found in the Gaudy Commodore (*Precis octavia*) and the Club-tailed Charaxes (*Charaxes zoolina*).

Many species of butterflies exhibit what is termed geographical or sub-specific variation, in which individual populations of a species, usually those isolated by some natural barrier, have developed slight differences which distinguish them from other populations of the same species. Geographical variation is marked amongst those butterflies which are confined to isolated forest areas. For example, in the species *Papilio ophidicephalus* and *Charaxes xiphares* a number of subspecies (or races as they are sometimes called) have evolved in the relic forests of southern Africa. In contrast those species which occur in a great variety of habitats and which have a more or less continuous distribution exhibit little or no geographical variation. Examples of such are *Papilio demodocus*, *Vanessa cardui* and *Catopsilia florella*.

Some butterflies possess distinctive wing shapes and colour patterns which blend into the surroundings when the insect is settled. This is termed cryptic coloration. A good example is the African Leaf Butterfly (*Kallima rumia*) which has an underside pattern and shape closely resembling a dead leaf, so that when resting on a twig it is extremely difficult to detect.

Other butterflies exhibit bright colours, especially vivid reds and black, and have a slow, buoyant flight; such species are reputedly distasteful to creatures which eat insects. The theory is that predators soon learn to associate the bright colours and leisurely flight with prey that is inedible. The Monarchs and the Acraeas, both of which families exude pungent juices when captured and handled, are examples of insects exhibiting what is called warning coloration.

Many species exhibiting warning coloration are mimicked both in colour and flight by certain edible butterflies which apparently derive protection from their close resemblance to their distasteful models. For example various females of the Mocker Swallowtail (*Papilio dardanus*) are very similar to certain of the Monarchs; the female of the Diadem (*Hypolimnas misippus*) closely resembles the African Monarch (*Danaus chrysippus*) and both sexes of the Nymphalid *Pseudacraea eurytus* are remarkably close mimics of the Acraea *Bematistes aganice*.

Many of the Blues possess long slender tails and hindwing lobes. When the butterfly is settled, usually head downwards with the wings closed, it moves its hindwings so that the tails resemble antennae and the lobes an insect's head. A bird or lizard predator is attracted by this movement, seizes what it thinks is the prey's head and the butterfly escapes.

The males of many butterflies, especially among the Swordtail Swallowtails, Browns, Monarchs and Blues, possess patches of modified scales or hairs which are scented, apparently to attract the female. These scent scale patches, or androconia as they are called, take the form of a band on the forewing in the Browns; a small black patch on the hindwing of the Monarchs; hairs inside the flap along the hindwing and margin in the Swordtail Swallowtails; and a rounded patch on the costal margin of the hindwing in some Blues.

Distribution

By far the richest region for lepidoptera on the African continent is in the low altitude West African rain forests, which extend eastwards across a major part of the Congo basin, with relic forest patches in Uganda and extreme western Kenya. The moist tropical climate and lush vegetation are extremely favourable to butterflies, permitting a rapid succession of broods without the check of wet and dry seasons or the prolonged droughts experienced spasmodically in more arid regions. The butterfly fauna, which exceeds one thousand species in some areas, is especially rich in Nymphalids and Lycaenids. Butterflies are on the wing throughout the year.

Highland forests, with the possible exception of the Ruwenzori–Kivu region, support a much less abundant butterfly fauna, but possess a restricted number of endemic species, some of which are of special interest. Whilst butterflies may be found throughout the year, peak abundance is during and immediately after the rainy seasons.

The moist woodland and savannah of central Africa, south to Rhodesia, are also relatively rich butterfly country: over 450 species have been recorded. Peak abundance is from October to March.

The coastal regions of East Africa, especially where forested, are seasonally rich in insect-life, but butterfly abundance is dependant on the rains which are sometimes unpredictable. April and May and late September and October are usually good months.

South Africa boasts a large number of endemic species amongst the 430-odd butterflies known to occur, but many of these are rare and extremely local. This applies especially to the many endemic Coppers, Blues and Browns. Whilst some butterflies may be found on the wing throughout the year in the warmer districts, they are most in evidence from September to April.

Equipment

Before starting to make a collection of butterflies certain items of equipment are necessary. The essentials are:

Butterfly net
Killing bottles
Curved entomological forceps
Butterfly envelopes and flat tin boxes
Plastic relaxing box and relaxing fluid
Entomological pins
Setting boards and transparent paper strips
Setting needle
Entomological store boxes
Naphthalene and/or paradichlorbenzene crystals.

Entomological Net

This may be purchased from a firm dealing in entomological supplies or it may be home-made. The most efficient type of net for use in Africa, one suitable for netting the largest swallowtails, is that known as a Kite Net. This has a frame measuring 24 inches long by 15 inches wide composed of two tubular metal side pieces, a brass Y-piece and a slightly flexible hoop; the sections fit together like a fishing rod. The net bag should be made of small-mesh, light-weight nylon netting, not of heavy mosquito netting, and should be 30 inches deep with a rounded bottom. Nets with squared corners result in damage to butterflies, especially the smaller species.

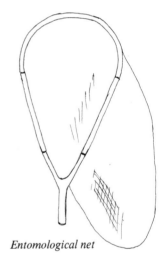

Entomological net

Such a net may be used either with or without a handle – a matter of personal choice, although a four or five ft. handle is recommended for capturing high-flying insects.

Among other types of net which may be purchased is a small net of 12 inches diameter, on a steel spring frame. It has the advantage of being folded or assembled in a matter of seconds, and when not in use can be carried in the pocket out of sight.

A home-made net should have a stout wire frame at least 15 inches in diameter. The net bag, bordered by a narrow casing of unbleached cotton or suchlike material which fits over the wire frame, should be about 30 inches deep. The ends of the wire frame are bound into the end of a three to four ft. handle.

The colour of the net is largely one of personal choice, but a white net has the advantage that the captured butterfly can be seen more clearly than through black or coloured netting.

Killing Bottles

Killing bottles are wide-mouthed jars with a tight screw-on cap; two sizes should be carried in the field. The ideal sizes are 4 inches high with a mouth diameter of $1\frac{1}{2}$ inches, and 6 inches high with a mouth diameter of 3 inches. Potassium cyanide is the normal killing agent and a cyanide killing bottle has the advantage of retaining its potency for a year or longer. But it *must* be remembered that cyanide is a deadly poison and care is necessary in its use.

To make a cyanide killing bottle place a $\frac{1}{2}$ inch layer of potassium cyanide lumps in the bottom of the jar and cover with half an inch of clean dry sawdust. Then mix up some plaster of paris to the consistency of thick cream and pour in a half inch layer over the sawdust. Leave the jar open in a garage or other well-ventilated place until the plaster is completely dry. This usually takes about two days. Then close with the screw cap. As an added precaution the killing jar should be bound with transparent adhesive tape to guard against breakage. The bottle must be labelled 'Deadly Poison – Cyanide' and kept out of reach of small children.

As an alternative to cyanide, using a killing agent harmless to humans, the ethyl acetate killing bottle is recommended. This is a jar containing an inch of plaster of paris. When the bottle is needed a teaspoonful of ethyl acetate is poured on to the plaster, into which it is absorbed. This is an excellent killing bottle but has the disadvantage that ethyl acetate evaporates quickly, necessitating recharging two or three times a day when in constant use.

Entomological Forceps

If damage to your specimens is to be avoided it is essential to use forceps in handling them. Several designs are sold by dealers in entomological supplies. Curved forceps with blunt, squared tips are recommended; these may be used for handling freshly collected specimens, dried butterflies in papers, and also pinned specimens. (*Below*)

Entomological forceps

Butterfly Envelopes

Square, semi-transparent paper envelopes with ungummed flaps, as sold by dealers in photographic supplies for the storage of negatives, are ideal for papering butterflies. The specimen's data is written on the flap, which is then folded over.

If negative envelopes are not available, triangular envelopes may be made from thin typing paper or even from newspaper. An ideal sized triangular envelope is made as follows: take a rectangular piece of paper measuring six by four inches; fold diagonally and then fold over the flaps to form a triangle. The butterfly is inserted into the envelope or triangle with wings folded above the back. Data concerning the specimen is written on the open flap which is then folded over. Data should include locality, date of capture, and name of collector. Triangles and negative envelopes are conveniently carried in the field in flat tin boxes.

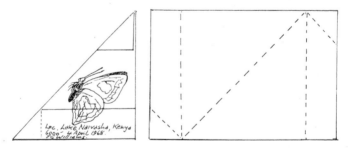

Folding and labelling triangular envelope for storing unset butterfly specimens

Relaxing Box and Relaxing Fluid

The relaxing box is an essential item of equipment. Prior to setting a butterfly (as described later) the specimen must be completely limp and relaxed. In several books dealing with the preparation of butterfly specimens it is stated that butterflies are in a satisfactory state for setting on the same day they are captured. This is not always the case. Specimens stiffen up quite soon after they have been killed and must be placed in a relaxing box overnight, when they become completely lax and easy to set.

The ideal relaxing box can be made from a plastic sandwich box with a close-fitting press-on lid. The box is lined with two or three layers of blotting paper, on to which – depending on the size of the box – one or two tea-spoonfuls of relaxing fluid are poured. A layer of absorbent cotton-wool is then placed on top and the box sealed. It is ready for use in about twelve hours. The cotton-wool should feel slightly damp to the touch, but not wet. Freshly caught specimens are laid on top of the cotton-wool, the box closed and left overnight. Specimens can be left in their papers and stored in larger plastic relaxing boxes for at least two weeks and still be in perfect condition for setting. Dry papered specimens may be relaxed in the same way, but take two or three days before they are ready for setting.

Relaxing fluid can be made up at any chemist's; it is a 1 in 1000 aqueous solution of thiomersalate.

Entomological Pins

Entomological pins must be purchased from dealers. Ordinary pins are quite unsuitable for mounting insects: and it is strongly recommended that only stainless steel pins be used. These pins are one and a half inches long and graded in various thicknesses. No. 1 size should be used for pinning the smallest butterflies such as Blues; no. 3 for medium-sized species such as Whites, and no. 5 for large, heavy-bodied butterflies such as the larger Charaxes. Pins are sold in two colours, black and 'white'. It is a question of personal preference which is used, but a black pin is less obvious than a white one.

Setting Boards and Accessories

The standard type of setting board has a plywood base, usually 12–14 inches long, which supports two narrower wooden blocks of equal width. These are separated by a gap or groove to take the insect's body. The upper blocks and the bottom of the groove are covered with sheet cork or cork composition, which in turn is covered with smooth white paper to avoid any roughness of surface which might damage a fragile butterfly's wings. The depth of the groove should be half an inch to allow the butterfly to be pinned high on the pin, so giving adequate space for the data label which is pinned below the insect.

A selection of setting boards of different widths is needed for pinning butterflies of different sizes. The most useful widths are 1 inch for very small butterflies, $1\frac{1}{2}$ inches, 2 inches, $2\frac{1}{2}$ inches, 3 inches and 4 inches.

Semi-transparent strips for holding the butterfly's wings in place on the setting board can be cut from sheets of thin tracing paper, or rolls of 'setting strips' of various widths can be purchased from a dealer in entomological supplies.

A setting needle is also needed, for raising the specimen's wings during the setting operation. This can be purchased or may be made from a three inch length of quarter inch wooden dowelling with a fine sewing needle set into one end. Care should be taken that the needle is in a straight line with the handle. In Africa an excellent and light-weight setting needle can be made by inserting a fine sewing needle into the blunt end of a short porcupine quill.

Entomological Store Boxes

The ideal method of storing a collection of butterflies is in cork-lined glass-topped drawers of a specially constructed insect cabinet. However, such a piece of furniture is expensive and usually beyond the means of the amateur collector. The alternative is to keep the specimens either in cork-lined wooden store boxes or in glass-topped display cases. These may be purchased from dealers in entomological supplies. The former cost approximately 30s to 50s each, depending on size; the latter, measuring 14 by 10 inches, are about 20s each. If glass-topped display cases are used these should be kept in the dark as strong sunlight will soon fade your specimens.

Naphthalene or paradichlorbenzene crystals must be kept in the boxes to repel the minute insect pests which would otherwise destroy your specimens. Store boxes usually have a camphor cell incorporated into one side of the box, in which to place the naphthalene crystals. In display cases without such camphor cells, the easiest way to protect your specimens is to pin one or two moth balls into a corner of the box. Paradichlorbenzene is a stronger pesticide than naphthalene but has the disadvantage of being highly volatile, needing replacement every few weeks.

Collecting

Most butterfly specimens are captured by netting: this being so it is important to learn to use a net correctly. Butterflies are seldom caught in a mad chase; and if they are, the specimens are often damaged by impinging forcibly against the net during the final lunge. Learn to approach carefully and to secure the insect, either in flight or when settled, by a rapid sweep with the mouth of the net held sideways. As the insect is netted continue the movement, at the same time twisting the wrist so that the mouth of the net faces downwards and the net bag hangs over the hoop imprisoning the specimen.

If the captured butterfly is very small, insert the mouth of your smaller killing bottle into the net, manoeuvre the insect inside and slip on the cap. As soon as it appears to be dead remove it with the forceps and place it inside a butterfly envelope. Transfer the envelope containing the specimen into your larger killing bottle for half an hour or more to ensure that it is dead.

Larger insects, from the size of a White upwards, are best dealt with initially by 'pinching' the thorax: they are then put straight into a butterfly envelope and placed in the large killing bottle. Pinching a butterfly's thorax must be done quickly before its fluttering causes damage. Corner the specimen between folds of the net with its wings together above the back, then with forefinger and thumb give the thorax a sharp squeeze. A little practice will indicate the correct pressure. When removing the specimen use forceps: the wings must not be handled with the fingers as this would dislodge scales and cause damage.

Always examine a captured insect before killing it; if it is damaged, or a species you do not need, let it go. Never put more than one butterfly into a killing bottle at one time, and don't carry a number of dead specimens loose in the killing bottle unpapered. They always rub against one another and become damaged.

During field trips visit as many different butterfly habitats as possible. The species found along forest roads will be different from those occurring, say, in acacia bush country: and collect in different seasons, a locality where there were few insects prior to the rains may be swarming with butterflies a couple of weeks after the rains have started.

Not all butterflies feed upon nectar from flowers. Males of the genus Charaxes, a group which includes some of the finest African butterflies, feed largely upon the juices of carnivore dung and may be attracted by fresh dog droppings. The females, and to some extent the males, feed on fermenting sap from tree trunks where borer beetles have been at work. Both sexes may be attracted to fermenting squashed bananas spread in patches on tree trunks.

Males of many Swallowtails, Whites, Acraeas and Blues are greatly attracted to patches of damp sand or gravel which have been moistened with urine – human or animal. At such spots the insects often gather in great swarms, and perfect specimens may be taken with ease.

Certain times of the day are more favourable than others for collecting high-flying Swallowtails such as *Papilio rex*. These butterflies frequently visit low-growing flowers in the early morning or late evening, but spend the rest of the day flying around the tops of forest trees well out of reach.

In bush country the tops of small hills have an attraction for many kinds of Blues, and other butterflies as well, which fly around and settle on bushes growing on the summit.

Breeding

One of the most rewarding methods of collecting butterflies is to breed them. Perfect specimens are obtained, details of early stages come under observation, and specimens not needed may be released. Breeding may be initiated in two ways: either eggs or larvae may be searched for on suitable food plants, brought home and reared through to the adult insect, or females of certain groups may be captured and placed in a laying cage with twigs of the larval food plant in water.

The first method is most successful if the collector is anxious to add specimens of *Iolaus* Blues to his collection. These most beautiful butterflies are difficult to net, many species keeping to the tree-tops. Different species lay their eggs – tiny, white, pitted half spheres – on the leaves, twigs and flowers of various species of *Loranthus*, a parasitic, mistletoe-like plant which grows on trees and bushes. The larvae are cryptically coloured, resembling sections of leaf of their food plant. However, a careful search of the food plant will reveal both ova and larvae, which may be reared in transparent plastic boxes sold for the purpose, renewing the food plant twice a week. It is important to have only one larva to one container, and the container must be kept very clean.

The second method is moderately successful with Swallowtails and those Charaxes in which the larval food plant is known. The female butterfly is put into a laying cage, with twigs of the larval food plant in a jar of water. The cage is a wooden frame on a wooden bottom, the sides and top covered with mosquito gauze, leaving slack at the top to be closed with a rubber band after the butterfly is inside. It must be large enough for the butterfly to fly freely. The ideal size for a swallowtail is 24 inches by 24 inches and 30 inches high. A smaller cage will often inhibit the butterfly from laying. The cage is suspended from the branch of a tree, half in shadow, half in sunshine.

It is necessary to feed the female butterfly twice a day whilst she is in captivity. To accomplish this hold the butterfly by her closed wings, uncoil her tongue with a needle or pin and guide the tongue tip on to a cube of sugar moistened with water. She will soon commence to feed and you can release your hold. Replace the food plant every two or three days with fresh foliage. As a rule the female does not commence laying for several days. The eggs when laid should be removed daily and kept in plastic boxes until they hatch.

The best and least troublesome method of rearing larvae is to enclose five or six in a sleeve of muslin slipped over a branch of the food plant and tied at both ends. This ensures the larvae a continuous supply of fresh food in natural conditions. Examine the sleeves at intervals to remove trash and when necessary transfer the larvae to fresh foliage. When the larvae have pupated the pupae may be removed and placed in the laying cage until the perfect insect emerges.

Setting

The completely lax specimen, taken from the relaxing box, is held from below with the thorax between forefinger and thumb of the left hand. An entomological pin of the correct size (see under heading Entomological Pins) is gripped by forceps and driven vertically through the centre of the thorax, the point emerging between the central pair of legs. The specimen is pushed half way up the pin, which is then inserted into the groove in the setting board.

With the aid of the setting needle the thorax is pushed down until the base of the wings is level with the top of the setting board. Then the body is straightened and held in place with a pin pushed into the groove against the left side of the abdomen to prevent body movement whilst setting the wings.

Next, two strips of thin tracing paper, each a little narrower than the top pieces of the setting board, are pinned longitudinally to the top of the board so that the edges lie just short of the groove and cover the butterfly's wings. Holding the paper with extended forefinger and thumb, the left hand wings, each in turn, are moved forward until the lower margin of the forewing is at

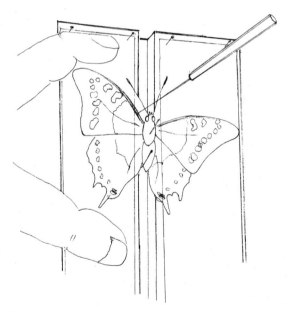

Setting a butterfly specimen

right angles to the body, leaving a small V-shaped gap between the fore and hindwings. Movement is achieved by pressing the point of the setting needle against the base of the thick veins, being careful neither to pierce the wings nor to touch them with the fingers. When the two wings are in correct position they are fixed by pinning the paper down all around the wings, but not through them.

The pin on the left hand side of the abdomen is now transferred to the right side, and the right wings set so that they balance those of the left. They are likewise secured by pinning down the paper strip around them, then the pin is removed from the right side of the abdomen. The antennae are now spread and kept in position with two or three pins. The data label is written and pinned on the board to the side of the specimen.

Specimens should remain on the setting boards until completely dry – a week to ten days in the case of smaller butterflies, up to three weeks for large ones. The setting boards with pinned specimens should be kept in a box or cupboard with naphthalene sprinkled around to discourage ants and other pests which might damage the specimens.

Labelling

A butterfly specimen without a data label has no scientific value. The label, written in Indian ink on thin card or high-grade paper, is pinned underneath the specimen. It should carry full details of locality in which the specimen was captured, date of collection and name of collector. It is important to give the locality in full. For example, a butterfly collected in the Karura Forest, Nairobi, Kenya, 5600 ft. must bear all this information: it is not enough to put 'Karura Forest' and leave it at that.

If the specimen was reared from egg or larva, a note that it was bred should appear on the reverse side of the label, together with name of food plant.

A data label should be as small as possible and the writing small and neat. If a large number of specimens are taken in one locality it is worth while to have a supply of labels printed so that you have only to fill in the date: or if smaller numbers of specimens are involved the data can be typed and then photographed down to the required size.

It is also a good practice to give your specimen a number, to correspond with an entry in your collector's record book. In this you can note details of habitat, descriptions of early stages and other information, which will greatly enhance the value of your collection. But do *not* use numbers on the specimens as a substitute for the data slip: note books do get lost and then the collection is valueless.

Sexing

It is always desirable to give the sex of the specimen on your data label or in your field notes.

To sex a butterfly examine the ventral surface of the end of the abdomen through a hand lens. In males the abdomen terminates in a pair of flattened appendages known as claspers, with which the male grips the tip of the female's abdomen during copulation: under the lens the space between these organs appears as a longitudinal slit. The female lacks claspers.

Collecting: Early Stages

The amateur entomologist can add much to scientific knowledge by collecting and preserving the early stages of African butterflies, many of which are still unknown. It is recommended that such be preserved in a fluid medium rather than as dry specimens, as then the entire anatomy is available for study. Examples of ova, larvae in all instars and pupae may be preserved in a weak formalin solution, one part of 40% commercial formalin to twenty parts water.

Ova are merely dropped into a small phial of the formalin solution together with a label. Larvae and pupae should first be placed in the killing bottle and then transferred to phials of preserving fluid. It is important to preserve the parent female butterfly, however damaged it may be, and to include identification of the species on the labels attached to all ova, larvae and pupae, in addition to other data such as locality and food plant.

In America larvae are usually preserved in a solution called Pempel's Fluid, which is made up of 15 parts 95% ethyl alcohol, 30 parts distilled water, 6 parts 40% formalin and 4 parts glacial acetic acid.

Papered Specimens

The amateur lepidopterist who is a visitor or temporary resident in Africa has the problem of transporting a bulky collection of set butterflies when he returns home. In such cases it is perhaps better to build up the collection as papered specimens, in negative envelopes or triangles, each with full data written on the flap. Such a collection takes up little space. The specimens are stored between thin layers of cotton wool in sealed cardboard or tin boxes, with a plentiful sprinkling of naphthalene to keep out insect pests. Papered specimens keep in perfect condition for years and can be relaxed and set at leisure.

Presentation of a Collection

A collection should be arranged in systematic sequence as far as is possible. Each species should be represented by two or three examples of each sex, plus a male and female mounted upside down to show the underside. In the case of those butterflies which exhibit great variation more than two or three specimens of each sex will be needed to illustrate this diversity. The specimens should be arranged in two rows, males on the left, females on the right, with the species' name printed on a card pinned below them.

Some Entomological Terms (*see figure below*)

♂ ♀	The signs used to denote male ♂ and female ♀
abdomen	The third section of the body of a butterfly (1)
anal angle	The lower inner angle of the hindwing (2)
androconia	Patches of specialized scent scales on the wings of certain male butterflies
antennae	A butterfly's 'feelers', arising from the head between the eyes: in nearly all African butterflies they are thickened or clubbed at the tips
apex	Tip of fore or hindwing; usually used in connection with forewing (3)

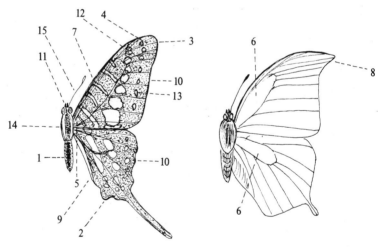

Topography of a butterfly, illustrating terms used in this volume

1 abdomen	6 cells	11 palps
2 anal angle (tornus)	7 costa	12 subapical
3 apex	8 falcate	13 submarginal
4 apical angle	9 inner angle	14 thorax
5 base	10 outer margin	15 antennae

apical angle   The upper (outer) angle of the wing; normally used in connection with forewing (4)

base   That portion of the wing nearest the thorax (5)

cells (wing)   Central section of wings surrounded but not crossed by veins (6)

cilia   Fringe of very short fine hairs along outer margins of wings

costa   Front margin of fore and hindwings (7)

cremaster   Hooks at anal end of pupa

crepuscular   Flying at dusk

cryptic coloration   Indicates butterfly is coloured or patterned in such a way that it is camouflaged when settled in normal habitat

dimorphism   When two examples of a single species differ from one another in form, colour or pattern. Sexual dimorphism when males and females are dissimilar; seasonal dimorphism when species exhibits differences in dry and wet season forms

distal   Outer portion of wings; away from body

diurnal   Flying during the day

dorsal surface   Upper surface of wings or body

d.s.f.   Dry season form

ecdysis   Larval moults

Ethiopian Region   Africa south of the Sahara

falcate   Where the wing apex is curved outwards and attenuated (8)

Family   Major group of butterflies consisting of related genera

forewings   Front pair of wings

frenulum   A coupling structure uniting fore and hindwings of moths in flight: absent in butterflies (*see figure* 1, *page* 11)

Genus (pl. genera)   A group of related species

girdle   Silken band round pupa which assists in support

Heterocera   General term used for moths

hindwings   Lower pair of wings

humeral lobe   Projection at base of hindwing costa in butterflies; serves to keep fore and hindwings together in flight, taking place of frenulum found in moths

hyaline   Clear, transparent

imago   Adult butterfly

inner angle	Lower angle of hindwing (9)
inner margin	Lower margin of hindwing; anal margin
instar	Stage of larval growth between moults
larva (pl. larvae)	Caterpillar
Lepidoptera	Insect Order to which butterflies and moths belong; scale-winged
lunule	Crescentic marking
mimicry	Resemblance of one species of insect to another species
outer margin	Outer margin of wings; distal margin (10)
palps	Pair of jointed, hairy processes, on each side of the base of the tongue (11)
polymorphism	Term used when one species or one sex exhibits great variety of forms: eg. ♀♀ of *Papilio dardanus*
proboscis	Butterfly's coiled tongue
proximal	Nearest to body
pupa (pl. pupae)	Chrysalis
Rhapalocera	General term used for butterflies
scales	Microscopic platelets which cover wings of butterflies and moths
scent scales	Patches of specialized scales or hairs on males of certain butterflies
serrated	Having a saw-like edge
subapical	Below but near to apex (12)
submarginal	Near margin (13)
thorax	Middle section of a butterfly's body (head, thorax, abdomen) to which wings and legs are attached (14)
tornus	Lower angle of a wing
translucent	Semi-transparent
undulate	Wavy
veins	Supporting struts of the wings
venation	Pattern of wing veins
ventral	Under surface of body or wings
warning coloration	Colours rendering an insect conspicuous, suggesting to potential enemies that it is distasteful
wing expanse	Width across the set butterfly from apex to apex
w.s.f.	Wet season form

FAMILY PAPILIONIDAE
SWALLOWTAILS

Members of this group include some of the largest and most beautiful of African butterflies. Many species are tailed. Characters of the Family include front legs fully developed in both sexes and the discoidal cell in both fore and hindwings closed distally. All are strong fliers, some flying high, others keeping nearer the ground. Most species are forest or woodland insects. Both sexes feed at flowers, and males are much attracted to wet mud or gravel and to soil moistened by urine.

Early Stages. The eggs are spherical, smooth, and laid singly or in small lots on leaves of the larval food plant. The larvae are smooth skinned and variable in appearance: they are remarkable in possessing a soft retractile forked horn just behind the head. When disturbed this organ is everted and emits a disagreeable odour. The pupae are angular with projections; they are attached by the tail and supported by a thin silken girdle.

PAPILIO ANTIMACHUS Drury
African Giant Swallowtail   p 36
Identification Wingspan ♂ 20–23cm.
♀ 15cm. Africa's largest butterfly,
characterised by its long narrow wings:

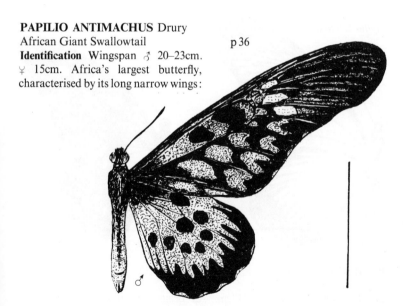

orange to reddish-brown with black markings, resembling a gigantic Acraea. ♀ has more rounded wings and is smaller.

Range and Habitat Forests of West Africa and the Congo, from Sierra Leone to western Uganda, where recorded from the Bwamba, Kibale, Kalinzu and Kayonza Forests. A rare insect in eastern part of its range; ♂♂ sometimes attracted to mud at the edge of forest pools and streams; ♀ very seldom encountered. Flies throughout year: Uganda specimens have been collected in January and in June.

PAPILIO ZALMOXIS Hewitson   p 36
Giant Blue Swallowtail

Identification Wingspan 14–15cm. A large tailless pale blue swallowtail with black vein streaks and a black border on hindwing; abdomen bright yellow. ♀ has greyish-blue hindwings with a yellowish wash in the cell.

Range and Habitat Forests of West Africa and the Congo. ♂♂ not uncommon in west of range and often found drinking on mud, but ♀ extremely rare and very few specimens exist in collections. Flies throughout the year.

Papilio zalmoxis

Papilio rex

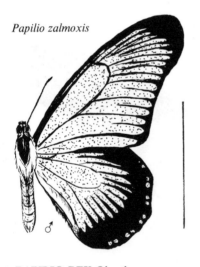

PAPILIO REX Oberthur   p 36
Regal Swallowtail

Identification Wingspan 10–12cm. An orange-brown or reddish-brown, black and white, tailless swallowtail. ♀ has more rounded forewings and more extensive orange-brown or reddish-brown at base of forewing.

Range and Habitat Occurs in highland forests of East Africa, Ethiopia, southern Sudan, eastern Congo and the Cameroons. Generally flies high around tree-tops, well out of range of a net, but may be taken at flowers in the early morning. Visits flowering bougainvillea in gardens adjacent to forest areas. Not uncommon in the forests around Nairobi, Kenya. Flies throughout year with a probable peak period during January.

Larval Food Plants Cape chestnut (*Calodendron capense*).

PAPILIO DARDANUS Brown   p 36
Mocker Swallowtail

Identification Wingspan 7–11cm. Sexes dissimilar. ♂ a pale creamy-yellow. tailed swallowtail with black forewing margin and varying amounts of black on hindwing. ♀♀ tailless except for races found in Ethiopia and Madagascar regions where they are tailed. Extremely variable in colour and pattern; mimics certain Danaid butterflies. May be black and white, black and orange, black, white and orange or black and creamy yellow.

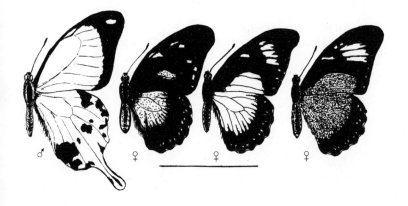

Range and Habitat Common in forested and wooded areas throughout Ethiopian Region, often visiting flowers in gardens. Flies usually within six feet of ground. ♀♀ tend to keep to semi-shade inside forest and are less often seen, but they are by no means rare. In South Africa *dardanus* is on the wing from October to April: further north it flies throughout the year.

Larval Food Plants These include cultivated *Citrus, Clausena, Toddalia, Teclea* and Cape chestnut (*Calodendron capense*).

PAPILIONIDAE – SWALLOWTAILS

1 **PAPILIO DARDANUS** ♂♀♀   *page* 35
   ♂ tailed, creamy yellow with black markings: ♀♀ tail-less except in
   Ethiopian and Madagascar races: extremely variable.

2 **PAPILIO CHAROPUS** ♂   43
   Sexes similar: tailed: broad blue band.

3 **PAPILIO REX** ♂   34
   Sexes similar but ♀ with rounder forewings. Mimics the Danaid,
   Melinda formosa.

4 **PAPILIO HORNIMANI** ♂   42
   Sexes similar: tailed: narrow blue band.

5 **PAPILIO ZALMOXIS** ♂   34
   ♀ has greyish-blue hindwings with yellowish wash in cell.

6 **PAPILIO ANTIMACHUS** ♂   33
   Largest African butterfly: ♀ smaller with rounded wings.

1 ♂ 1 ♀ 1 ♀ 2 ♂ 3 ♂ 4 ♂ 5 ♂ 6 ♂

PLATE 2   37

PAPILIONIDAE – SWALLOWTAILS

1 **PAPILIO CONSTANTINUS** ♂   *page* 38
Sexes similar: large yellow spot in forewing cell.

2 **PAPILIO NOBILIS** ♀♂   39
Bright yellow with red-brown markings.

3 **PAPILIO PHORCAS** ♀♂   38
Two forms of ♀, one similar to ♂, the other with brownish-yellow band.

4 **PAPILIO HESPERUS** ♂   40
Sexes similar: usually three yellow spots on hindwing.

5 **PAPILIO MACKINNONI** ♂   42
Sexes similar: golden-yellow spots forming broken band.

6 **PAPILIO THURAUI** ♂   46
Sexes similar: black with submarginal blue spots on both wings.

7 **PAPILIO LEUCOTAENIA** ♂   48
♀ resembles ♂ but paler, with broader band: tailed: greenish-white
median band.

PAPILIO CONSTANTINUS Ward   p 37
Constantine's Swallowtail

Identification Wingspan 9–11cm. A dark brown, tailed swallowtail with pale yellow markings: differs from *P. euphranor* in having an oval yellow patch in the cell of the forewing. ♀ resembles ♂ but tends to have more extensive yellow markings and is often larger.

Range and Habitat Occurs in open forest, woodland and coastal scrub. Ranges from South Africa (Natal and northern Transvaal) northwards through Mozambique, Rhodesia, Malawi and Zambia to Tanzania, Kenya and Ethiopia: also recorded from Katanga, Congo. Especially common in Kenya coastal forests. Flies within a few feet of the ground and feeds at low-growing flowers in undergrowth: ♀♀ keep to semi-shade and are less often seen than ♂♂. In the south flies from September to February; further north on wing throughout year. Along East African coast commonest during March–April and September–October.

PAPILIO PHORCAS Cramer   p 37
Green-patch Swallowtail

Identification Wingspan 8–10cm. A tailed black swallowtail with a bright green band on the forewing and a triangular green patch on the hindwing. There are two forms of ♀; one resembles the ♂ but has more extensive submarginal green spots on the fore and hindwings, the other is dark brown with a brownish-yellow discal band and large brownish-yellow submarginal spots. A rare variety sometimes occurs, both ♂ and ♀, in which the bright green bands and patches are replaced by greenish-cream.

Range and Habitat Occurs in forested and wooded areas throughout the Ethiopian Region north of the Zambesi, but not in Ethiopia. Very common in forests of Kenya, Uganda and the Congo. A relatively weak flier, keeping usually near the ground and feeding at low-growing flowers. On the wing throughout the year.

Larval Food Plants *Teclea*.

PAPILIO NOBILIS Rogenhofer   p 37
Noble Swallowtail

Identification Wingspan 9–11cm. A bright ochre-yellow, tailed swallow-tail with reddish-brown markings: ♀ resembles ♂ but is more heavily marked with reddish-brown. Some examples of a race occurring in western Uganda and the Kivu Province of the Congo have the brown markings in the ♂ replaced by whitish-grey.

Range and Habitat A mountain and highlands forest butterfly found in Kenya (where common around Nairobi), Uganda, northern Tanzania, the southern Sudan, Rwanda and Burundi. ♂♂ fly high but may be attracted

low by a dead specimen pinned to a branch, or even by a piece of orange-coloured paper. ♀♀ very uncommon, but sometimes found feeding at flowers in the early morning.
Larval Food Plants *Wahlbergia*.

PAPILIO HESPERUS Westwood   p 37
Black and Yellow Swallowtail
Identification Wingspan 11–12½cm. A large black and pale yellow tailed swallowtail with usually three yellow submarginal spots on hindwing. ♀ resembles ♂ but larger and has an orange spot in the tornus of the hindwing. The closely allied *P. pelodorus* has usually five yellow submarginal spots on hindwing, and both sexes have one or two orange spots at the tornus of the hindwing.

Range and Habitat A West African forest butterfly which ranges through the Congo to southern Sudan, Uganda and north-western Zambia. A strong flier, on the wing throughout the year, and difficult to capture unless drinking on mud. ♀♀ very uncommon, keeping to forest undergrowth.

PAPILIO PELODORUS Butler
Eastern Black and Yellow Swallowtail
Identification Wingspan 11–12cm. A distinctive black and yellow tailed swallowtail with five or six large yellow submarginal spots, and one or two

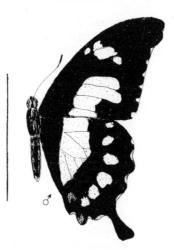

orange spots at the angle of the hindwing. ♀ like ♂ but with larger yellow spots and large orange spots in angle of hindwing. *P. hesperus* has usually three submarginal spots and ♂ lacks orange spot at the angle of the hindwing. **Range and Habitat** Mountain forests in eastern and southern Tanzania (where not uncommon near Lushoto in the western Usambara Mts.), south to Malawi. A strong flier, difficult to net unless drinking at muddy patch on road through forest. On the wing at any time of the year, but most frequent December–January and April–May.

PAPILIO EUPHRANOR Trimen
Bush Kite Swallowtail
Identification Wingspan 10–12cm.
A dark brown and yellow tailed
swallowtail somewhat resembling
P. constantinus, from which it
differs in its wider discal bands and
in lacking the yellow cell spot in
forewing. ♀ resembles ♂ but has
better developed submarginal
spots.
Range and Habitat Confined to
forested and wooded areas in
South Africa, being recorded from

Cape Province, Natal and Transvaal. Not uncommon in Ngei Forest near Kokstad, Cape Province. This is a high-flying butterfly, ♂♂ frequenting sunny forest glades and the outskirts of forest; in habits quite unlike *P. constantinus* which flies near the ground. On the wing from October to February.

p 37

PAPILIO MACKINNONI E. Sharpe
Mackinnon's Swallowtail
Identification Wingspan 9–11cm. A tailed blackish-brown swallowtail with a broken band of golden-yellow spots across fore and hindwings. ♀ resembles ♂ but usually with heavier spots.
Range and Habitat Found in highland forests of East Africa, south through eastern Congo to Zambia and Angola. Common in forests and wooded areas of Kenya especially around Nairobi. Has habit of flying backwards and forwards over a particular area, five or six feet above the ground. Flies throughout the year.
Larval Food Plants Noted laying on Cape chestnut (*Calodendron capense*).

PAPILIO HORNIMANI Distant
Horniman's Swallowtail

p 36

Identification Wingspan 9–10cm. A tailed black swallowtail with a metallic blue median band and blue submarginal spots: below blackish with band of silvery submarginal spots on hindwing. ♀ resembles ♂ but blue discal band duller and below lacks silvery submarginal spots. *P. charopus* of the Congo and western Uganda is smaller with much broader blue discal band, and below lacks silvery spots in both sexes.

Range and Habitat Highland forests of northern Tanzania and south-eastern Kenya. Locally not uncommon Chyulu Hills forests, south-eastern Kenya, and on Mt. Meru, Mt. Kilimanjaro and western Usambara Mts., Tanzania. On wing most of year but most frequent after rains, December–January and April–May. ♂♂ often attracted to mud and soil dampened by elephant urine. ♀♀ appear much rarer than ♂♂, but sometimes found feeding at flowers in early morning.

Larval Food Plants ♀♀ observed fluttering amongst *Teclea* foliage, apparently laying.

PAPILIO CHAROPUS Westwood
p 36

Westwood's Swallowtail

Identification Wingspan 8–9cm. A tailed black swallowtail with a broad blue median band. ♀ resembles ♂ but blue discal band usually duller. *Papilio hornimani* has a much narrower median band and occurs outside the range of *Papilio charopus*.

Range and Habitat Forests of West Africa and Congo, eastwards to western Uganda, where most frequent in forests near Fort Portal. ♂♂ are attracted to damp mud but ♀ is seldom seen. Flies throughout the year but commoner after rains.

PAPILIO AETHIOPS Rothschild & Jordan

Abyssinian Blue-banded Swallowtail

Identification Wingspan 8cm. A black swallowtail with a restricted blue median band: untailed but with lobed hindwings; forewing without white submarginal dots; blue median band on forewing of constant width; hindwing band relatively narrow.

Range and Habitat Forested areas of Ethiopia and Somalia; local and generally uncommon.

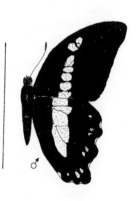

PAPILIONIDAE – SWALLOWTAILS

1 **PAPILIO LORMIERI** ♂   *page* 49
   Sexes similar: forewing band straight.

2 **PAPILIO NIREUS NIREUS** ♂♀   48
   Edges of blue median band irregular: usually no blue submarginal
   spots on forewing.

3 **PAPILIO MENESTHEUS** ♂   49
   Sexes similar: forewing band curved.

4 **PAPILIO OPHIDICEPHALUS** ♂   50
   Sexes similar: yellow median bands broad.

5 **PAPILIO DEMODOCUS** ♂   50
   Sexes similar: tailless.

6 **PAPILIO BROMIUS** ♂   46
   Sexes similar: broad blue median band: whitish submarginal spots
   underside forewing not well developed or even lacking, except in
   Kenya Highlands race, *P. b. chrapkowskii.*

7 **PAPILIO SOSIA** ♂   47
   Sexes similar: greenish-blue median band with straight edges: small
   blue submarginal spots on forewing.

8 **PAPILIO MAGDAE** ♂   47
   Sexes similar: vivid blue broad median band: large white submarginal
   spots underside forewing.

9 **PAPILIO NIREUS LYAEUS** ♂   48
   Sexes similar: narrower blue median band than *P. nireus nireus.*

PLATE 4   45

PAPILIONIDAE – SWALLOWTAILS

1   **PAPILIO JACKSONI** ♂♀   *page* 55
    ♂ narrow white median band: ♀ forewing, white apical spot set in from
    wing tip.

2   **PAPILIO ZOROASTRES** ♂♀   57
    ♂ white spot in cell of forewing: ♀ ochreous hindwing patch small.

3   **PAPILIO ECHERIOIDES** ♂♀   54
    ♂ no white spot in cell of forewing: ♀ forewing, white apical spot on
    wing tip.

4   **GRAPHIUM SIMONI** ♂   61
    Sexes similar: closely related *G. ucalegon*, plate 5, but pale markings
    white not buff.

5   **PAPILIO CYNORTA** ♂♀   53
    ♂ very broad straight white median band: ♀ variable, mimics
    Bematistes epaea (Acraeidae): pale areas may be white or
    ochreous-yellow.

6   **PAPILIO ZENOBIA** ♂   52
    Sexes similar: broad even median band.

7   **PAPILIO MECHOWI** ♂   51
    Sexes similar, but ♀ has broader median band: hindwing sharply
    angled: scent scale patches not apparent on forewing of ♂.

8   **PAPILIO GALLIENUS** ♂   51
    Sexes similar: hindwing less sharply angled than in *P. mechowi*: scent
    scale patches present on forewing of ♂.

9   **PAPILIO MECHOWIANUS** ♂   52
    Sexes similar: broad, curved white median band.

PAPILIO THURAUI Karsch
Blue-spotted Black Swallowtail

p 37

Identification Wingspan 7–8cm.
A tailless black swallowtail
with submarginal blue spots on
both wings. Sexes alike, but ♀
usually with larger blue spots.
Range and Habitat Confined to
mountain forests in southern
Tanzania and Malawi. Ex-
tremely local and usually uncommon, perhaps most fre-
quent in forests of Uhehe high-
lands, south of Iringa, Tanzania. Usually flies between March and September,
but appearances depend on rains.

PAPILIO BROMIUS Doubleday
Broad Blue-banded Swallowtail

p 44

Identification Wingspan 8–9cm. A
black, tailless swallowtail with a broad
median blue band. Sexes similar but ♀
duller. Underside blackish, often with
silky sheen; no whitish submarginal
spots on forewing except in races (*P. b.
chrapkowskii* and *P. b. ufipa*) found
in highlands of Kenya and S.-W.
Tanzania; hindwing often with purplish mottling. The very similar
Papilio magdae (=*brontes*) has a much
bluer median band, and large white
submarginal spots on underside of
forewing; purplish mottling on underside of hindwing absent. *Papilio sosia*
has a narrower and much greener blue
band of even width and straight edges. *Papilio nireus* has a much narrower,
greenish-blue band.
Range and Habitat A common butterfly in the forests of West Africa and the
Congo, ranging eastwards to Uganda and the highland forests of Kenya:
isolated populations in south-western Tanzania (Ufipa plateau) and Malawi
(Nyika plateau). Flies throughout the year over most of its range.
Larval Food Plants *Teclea* and probably other Rutaceae.

PAPILIO MAGDAE Gifford (=brontes) p44
Godman's Swallowtail

Identification Wingspan 8–9cm. A black tailless swallowtail with a broad, very bright, blue median band: sexes similar but ♀ often with larger submarginal spots on hindwing. Underside with large white submarginal spots on forewing: no purplish mottling on hindwing. Very similar to Kenya Highlands and south-western Tanzania races of *Papilio bromius* but blue median band much bluer and brighter. *Papilio sosia* has narrower and greener blue band of even width and with straight edges. *Papilio nireus* has a narrower band, also greenish-blue.

Range and Habitat Occurs in forest and wooded areas of south-eastern Kenya (Chyulu and Teita Hills) and highland areas of Tanzania and Malawi. In north of range flies throughout the year, commonest during and after rains: in the south appears mainly from December to May.

PAPILIO SOSIA Rothschild & Jordan p44
Straight-banded Swallowtail

Identification Wingspan 8–9cm. A black, tailless swallowtail with a greenish-blue, straight-edged median band of even width: small blue submarginal dots along outer edge of forewing. Underside blackish, without white submarginal spots on forewing, but with some small white marginal dots. Sexes similar, but median band sometimes greener in ♀. *Papilio nireus* has a narrower and more irregular median band.

Range and Habitat A West African forest species ranging across the Congo to Uganda, where local and uncommon; most frequent in forests along Tororo–Jinja road. Flies throughout the year.

PAPILIO NIREUS Linnaeus
Narrow Blue-banded Swallowtail
Identification Wingspan 8–10cm. A
black, tailless swallowtail with a
narrow irregular median band. Sexes
similar but ♀ often with greener, duller
median band and heavier submarginal
spots. The eastern and southern race,
P. n. lyaeus (p. 44) has a narrower blue
band and is smaller. The race found in
Ethiopia and Somalia, *P. n. pseudo-
nireus*, has the median band even narrower and reduced. *Papilio sosia* has
a straight-edged greenish-blue median
band of even width. *Papilio bromius*

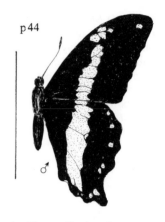

p 44

and *Papilio magdae* have brighter blue and much wider median bands.
Range and Habitat A common species throughout the Ethiopian Region in
forested, wooded and savannah country. The nominate race occurs in West
Africa, eastwards through the Congo to extreme western Uganda. *P. n. lyaeus*
occurs throughout eastern and southern Africa. In South Africa flies mainly
between September and April: elsewhere on the wing throughout the year.
Larval Food Plants Feeds on citrus, Cape chestnut (*Calodendron capense*),
Teclea and other Rutaceae.

PAPILIO LEUCOTAENIA Rothschild
Cream-banded Swallowtail
Identification Wingspan 9–10cm. A
dark blackish-grey, tailed swallowtail
with a greenish-white median band
and deeply scalloped wings. Underside variegated with browns, greys,
greens and black. Sexes similar but ♀
paler with broader median band.
Range and Habitat A rare species
found locally in mountain forests of
south-western Kigezi, Uganda and
adjacent areas of the Kivu, Rwanda
and Burundi. Sometimes not rare in
the Impenetrable Forest, south-
western Uganda, where it has the habit
of flying along margins of roadways

p 37

through the forest, but elusive and difficult to capture. Flies throughout the year, possibly most frequent during June and July.

PAPILIO MENESTHEUS Drury
Drury's Emperor Swallowtail
Identification Wingspan 6–10 cm. A large blackish tailed swallowtail peppered with yellow, with a yellow median band and yellow submarginal spots: yellow forewing band curved: hindwing with two eyespots marked with orange and blue: underside paler. Sexes alike but ♀ usually larger. *Papilio lormieri* has the forewing band straight, not curved; *Papilio ophidicephalus* has a much wider median band.
Range and Habitat Occurs in West African forests from Sierra Leone to the Cameroons. Flies throughout the year.

p 44

PAPILIO LORMIERI Distant
Western Emperor Swallowtail
Identification Wingspan 10–13 cm. A large blackish, tailed swallowtail, peppered with yellow and with a narrow yellow median band; band on forewing straight; hindwing with orange and blue marked eyespots. Sexes alike but ♀ usually larger. The closely related *Papilio menestheus* has the forewing band curved: *Papilio ophidicephalus* has a wide median band.
Range and Habitat A forest butterfly found in the Cameroons and Nigeria, south to

p 44

Angola, east through the Congo to Uganda and western Kenya. Not uncommon along roads through forest but ♀♀ less frequently encountered than ♂♂. Flies throughout the year.

Larval Food Plants Larvae have been recorded on *Fagara macrophylla*, citrus, *Vepris* and *Clausena anisata*.

PAPILIO OPHIDICEPHALUS Oberthur   p 44
Emperor Swallowtail

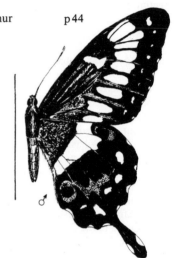

Identification Wingspan 10–14 cm. A very large tailed swallowtail, blackish peppered with yellow with a broad clear yellow median band: two eyespots marked with orange and blue on hindwing. Sexes alike but ♀ usually larger. The wider forewing band distinguishes this species from *Papilio menestheus* and *Papilio lormieri*.

Range and Habitat Forested country from eastern Kenya, south through Tanzania, Zambia and Mozambique to South Africa. In South Africa on the wing from September to April, with peaks in October and February. Further north flies throughout the year.

Larval Food Plants Larvae recorded on *Clausena* and citrus.

PAPILIO DEMODOCUS Esper   p 44
Citrus Swallowtail

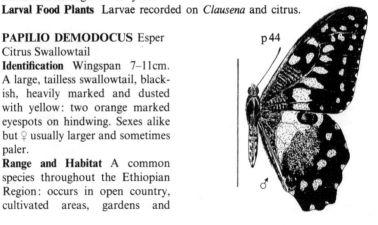

Identification Wingspan 7–11cm. A large, tailless swallowtail, blackish, heavily marked and dusted with yellow: two orange marked eyespots on hindwing. Sexes alike but ♀ usually larger and sometimes paler.

Range and Habitat A common species throughout the Ethiopian Region: occurs in open country, cultivated areas, gardens and forest margins. Probably the most abundant African swallowtail. In South Africa it is commonest from September to April. Further north it flies throughout the year.

Larval Food Plants Various cultivated citrus are the favoured food plant, but also found on Cape chestnut (*Calodendron capense*), *Clausena*, *Teclea*, *Bubon*, *Vepris*, *Toddalia* and *Hippobromus*.

PAPILIO MECHOWI Dewitz   p 45
Mechow's Swallowtail

Identification Wingspan 9–11cm. A large, tailless swallowtail, dark rich brown with a rich yellow median band: hindwing sharply angled, with large yellow marginal spots. Sexes similar but median band wider in ♀. The very similar *Papilio gallienus* has a less sharply angled hindwing, and in the male has conspicuous scent scale patches lying between the median band spots of the forewing: in *Papilio mechowi* these scent scales are not apparent.

Range and Habitat Forests and woodlands of the Cameroons, southern and eastern Congo, Angola, southern Sudan and Uganda, where it is not uncommon in the Budongo Forest. Flies throughout the year.

PAPILIO GALLIENUS Distant   p 45

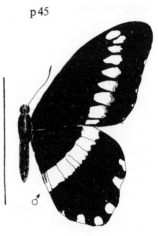

Identification Wingspan 9–11cm. A large tailless swallowtail, dark brown with a yellow median band: conspicuous patches of scent scales between median band spots on forewing in ♂. Sexes similar but median band wider in ♀. Hindwing less sharply angled than closely related *Papilio mechowi*, the ♂ of which lacks forewing scent scale patches.

Range and Habitat An uncommon forest species found in southern Nigeria and in the Congo. Flies throughout the year.

PAPILIO ZENOBIUS Godart
Identification Wingspan 8–10cm. A
dark brownish-black tailless swallowtail with a yellowish median
band (white in race found in Cameroons to Angola). The patches
forming the forewing band angular
on outer side. Yellow spots on
margin of fore and hindwings.
Sexes similar. *Papilio zenobia* lacks
distinct yellow spots on margin of
wings.
Range and Habitat A West African
forest species found in Sierra
Leone, the Congo and south to
Angola. Flies throughout the year.

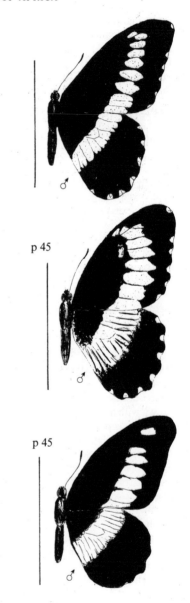

p 45

PAPILIO MECHOWIANUS Dewitz
Identification Wingspan 9–11cm.
A large blackish-brown tailless
swallowtail with broad pure white
median band. Band on forewing
curved inwards. Sexes similar but
median band wider in ♀.
Range and Habitat A West African
forest butterfly found from Liberia
to Angola and in the Congo. Flies
throughout the year.

p 45

PAPILIO ZENOBIA Fabricius
Identification Wingspan 8½–10cm.
A tailless black swallowtail with a
broad white median band, broader
in the ♀: usually no marginal white
spots on hindwing, or if present
very small. *Papilio zenobius* has
well-marked white or yellowish
marginal spots. *Papilio mechowianus* has a much broader and
curved median band.

Range and Habitat A forest swallowtail found in Sierra Leone, the Congo and western Uganda. Flies throughout the year.

PAPILIO ANDRONICUS Ward

Identification Wingspan 9–11cm. A large, blackish-brown tailless swallowtail with a very broad pure white median band. Sexes similar but band wider in ♀ and a white patch in upper angle of cell. The somewhat similar *Papilio mechowianus* has the forewing band curved inwards.

Range and Habitat An uncommon forest swallowtail found in the Cameroons, West Africa. Flies throughout the year.

PAPILIO CYNORTA Fabricius   p 45

Identification Wingspan 7–8½cm. ♂ a black tailless swallowtail with a broad creamy-white median band: hindwing white marginal spots very small. ♀ variable, mimics various forms of *Bematistes* (Acraeidae). The main forms are: blackish with pale markings white; dark brown, pale areas of forewing white, hindwing ochreous; all pale areas ochre-yellow; all pale markings much reduced, white and/or ochre.

Range and Habitat Forests of West Africa from Sierra Leone south to Angola, east through Congo to Uganda and western Kenya; an isolated population in Ethiopia. Flies throughout the year.

Larval Food Plants *Vepris* (Rutaceae).

PAPILIO PLAGIATUS Aurivillius

Identification Wingspan 7½–8½cm. ♂ a medium-sized blackish-brown tailless swallowtail with a pure white median band. ♀ with extensive white markings. Similar to *Papilio cynorta* but differs in both sexes in having outer margin of forewing concave, not straight or convex as in *Papilio cynorta*.

Range and Habitat Forests of the Cameroons and Nigeria, eastwards to northern Congo and southern Sudan. Flies throughout the year.

PAPILIO ECHERIOIDES Trimen　　　　　　　　　　　　　　p 45
White-banded Swallowtail

Identification Wingspan 7½–8½cm. ♂ a black tailless swallowtail with creamy-white median band: no white spot in cell of forewing. Differs from ♂ *Papilio cynorta* in having forewing median band tapering towards apex: ♀ mimics *Amauris echeria* and *A. albimaculata* (Danaidae), blackish-brown with white markings on hindwing. Differs from ♀ *Papilio jacksoni* in having white apical spot on margin. The similar ♀ *Papilio zoroastres* has a smaller ochreous patch on hindwing.

Range and Habitat Forest areas of Ethiopia, southwards through eastern Kenya and Tanzania to Zambia, Malawi, Rhodesia and Natal, South Africa. Flies near the ground and attracted to low-growing flowering plants. In South Africa on the wing from September to April; further north flies throughout the year but commonest during and after rains.

Larval Food Plants Reputed to lay on *Teclea* and Cape chestnut (*Calodendron capense*). In Malawi on *Toddalia*, *Clausena inaequalis* and *Fagara capensis*.

PAPILIO JACKSONI E. Sharpe   p45
Jackson's Swallowtail

Identification Wingspan 8–9cm. A sooty-brown, tailless swallowtail with a whitish median band, reduced to well separated spots on forewing with conspicuous scent scale patches in between. ♂ mimics *Amauris* sp. (Danaidae) dark brown with white markings on forewing and ochreous patch on hindwing. Differs from ♀ *Papilio echerioides* in having forewing apical white spot set in from margin.

Range and Habitat Occurs in highland and mountain forests in Kenya, Uganda and eastern Congo. Common in forests around Nairobi, Kenya, where it flies with *Papilio echerioides*. On the wing throughout the year, but commonest during and after rains.

Larval Food Plants Has been seen laying on *Teclea* (Rutaceae).

PAPILIO FULLEBORNI Karsch
Fulleborn's Swallowtail

Identification Wingspan 8–9cm. ♂ a deep black, tailless swallowtail with a pure white median band, very narrow on forewing, very wide on hindwing.

Easily distinguished from ♂ *Papilio jacksoni* by wide median band on hind-wing. ♀ mimics *Amauris* (Danaidae), blackish with white spotted forewing and ochreous patch on hindwing. Differs from ♀ *Papilio echerioides* in having marginal, not submarginal, spots on hindwing.

Range and Habitat Mountain forests of central and southern Tanzania: also recorded from mountain forest in Malawi.

PAPILIO SJOSTEDTI Aurivillius
Kilimanjaro Swallowtail

Identification Wingspan 9–10cm. ♂ a blackish-brown, tailless swallowtail with very narrow white median band: no submarginal white spots on hind-wing. ♀ resembles ♀ *Papilio fulleborni* but ochreous hindwing patch much smaller. Underside in both sexes much darker than in related species.

Range and Habitat Confined to mountain forest on Mt. Kilimanjaro and Mt. Meru in northern Tanzania. Flies throughout the year, but commonest during and after rains.

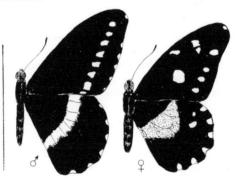

PAPILIO ZOROASTRES Druce
p 45

Identification Wingspan 7½–8½cm. ♂ a medium-sized, tailless swallowtail, blackish-brown with a white median band: differs from all related species in having a whitish spot in the cell of the forewing. ♀ with very small ochreous patch on hindwing.

Range and Habitat Forests of the Cameroons, Angola, Fernando Po, the Congo, eastwards to south-eastern Sudan, Uganda, north-west Tanzania and western Kenya. Flies throughout the year.

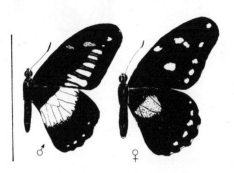

GRAPHIUM MORANIA Angas
White Lady Swallowtail

Identification Wingspan 6½–7cm. A relatively small tailless, black and white swallowtail: kidney-shaped white patch at apex of forewing cell. Sexes alike. The larger *Papilio pylades* lacks the white kidney-shaped patch and has fewer submarginal spots on hindwing.

Range and Habitat This is a southern species found in Rhodesia, Mozambique and Natal and Transvaal in South Africa, westwards to northern South-West Africa and Ovampoland. Inhabits savannah woodland, open country, bush and forest margins. In the south of its range flies mainly from late August to early May.

Larval Food Plants *Anona* (Anonaceae).

GRAPHIUM TABORANUS Oberthur
Tabora Swallowtail

Identification Wingspan 7–8 cm. A relatively small, tailless swallowtail, black with white markings and an orange patch near anal angle of hindwing. ♀ has white markings much reduced. Underside base of both wings crimson. Sides of abdomen black and white, not orange-yellow as in *Graphium pylades*.

Range and Habitat Found in open country, bush and woodland from Angola to southern Congo and Zambia, Malawi and Tanzania. Flies throughout the year but most frequent during and after rainy seasons.

Larval Food Plants *Anona* (Anonaceae).

GRAPHIUM PYLADES Fabricius
Angola White Lady Swallowtail

Identification Wingspan 8–10cm. A black and white, tailless swallowtail with an orange spot at tornus of hindwing; sides of abdomen orange-yellow: sexes alike. Differs from *Graphium morania* in lacking kidney-shaped white patch at apex of cell in forewing. *Graphium taboranus* has sides of abdomen black and white.

Range and Habitat Occurs in open country, bush and woodland; common throughout African continent in suitable habitats. Flies from April to September in south, throughout the year further north.

Larval Food Plants *Anona* (Anonaceae).

GRAPHIUM RIDLEYANUS White   p 64
Acraea Swallowtail

Identification Wingspan 7½–8½cm. A tailless black and red swallowtail which mimics some of the larger acraeas. Sexes similar, but ♀ usually with rounder wings: some ♀♀ have pale greyish-brown markings in place of red.

Range and Habitat Inhabits West African forests from Sierra Leone to Angola, the Congo and Uganda. ♂♂ attracted to wet mud, often associated with various acraeas which they resemble both in appearance and manner of flight. ♀ much less frequently seen than ♂. Flies throughout the year.

p 64

GRAPHIUM TYNDERAEUS Fabricius
Green-spotted Swallowtail

Identification Wingspan 7–8½cm. A black tailless swallowtail with bright green or yellowish-green markings: green sub-marginal spots present on forewing: hindwing deeply scalloped. Sexes similar, but ♀ usually with yellowish-green markings.

Range and Habitat A West African forest swallowtail found from Sierra Leone southwards, and in the Congo. A strong flier, not easy to capture on the wing. ♀ much rarer than ♂. Flies throughout the year.

p 64

GRAPHIUM LATREILLIANUS Godart
Coppery Swallowtail

Identification Wingspan 7–8½ cm. ♂ a black tailless swallow-tail with pale green to coppery-green markings: no green sub-marginal spots in forewing. ♀ differs in having smaller markings which are cream, not green. Underside in both sexes heavily washed with metallic copper.

Range and Habitat A West African forest species found in Sierra Leone to Angola, east-

wards through the Congo to extreme western Uganda (Bwamba Forest). Flies throughout the year.

GRAPHIUM HACHEI Dewitz

Identification Wingspan $6\frac{1}{2}$–$8\frac{1}{2}$ cm. A relatively small black swallowtail with a very broad white median band: apex of forewings pale. Sexes alike.

Range and Habitat An uncommon forest species found in the Cameroons, Angola and the Congo. Flies throughout the year.

GRAPHIUM UCALEGON Hewitson

p 64

Identification Wingspan 8–9cm. A small dark brown swallowtail with a broad ochreous median band. Sexes similar. *Graphium simoni* resembles this species in pattern but has the median band white.

Range and Habitat Inhabits forests of Nigeria, eastwards through the Congo to Uganda, where it is not uncommon in the Bwamba Forest, Toro. Flies throughout the year.

GRAPHIUM WEBERI Holland

Weber's Swallowtail

Identification Wingspan 8cm. A small tailless swallowtail, blackish-brown with pale ochreous markings: pale band much reduced: submarginal spots present. Underside pale chocolate with reddish base. Sexes alike.

Range and Habitat A very uncommon forest swallowtail found in the Cameroons.

GRAPHIUM AURIGER Butler

Identification Wingspan 8–9cm. A small tailless swallowtail, blackish with a white median band approximately 10mm. wide. Elongated pale patch in cell of forewing: subapical patches deeply serrated. Underside of hindwings intense black at base. Sexes alike.

Range and Habitat An uncommon forest swallowtail recorded from the Gabon, West Africa.

GRAPHIUM SIMONI Aurivillius   p 45
Simon's Swallowtail

Identification Wingspan 8–9cm. A relatively small tailless swallowtail, blackish-brown with a wide white median band: white triangular patch in cell of forewing. In pattern similar to *Graphium ucalegon*, but black and white, not brown and ochreous. Sexes alike.

Range and Habitat An uncommon and local forest swallowtail found in the Cameroons and the Congo. Flies throughout the year.

GRAPHIUM UCALEGONIDES Staudinger

Identification Wingspan 8–9cm. A medium-sized tailless swallowtail, brown with creamy-yellow or ochreous markings. Pattern differs from that of closely related *Graphium ucalegon* and *Graphium simoni*.

Range and Habitat A forest swallowtail found in West Africa from Ghana to the Cameroons and Angola, and in the Congo.

GRAPHIUM FULLERI Grose-Smith
Fuller's Swallowtail
Identification Wingspan 8–9cm.
A medium-sized tailless swallowtail, brown with yellowish
markings. Differs from *Graphium ucalegonides* in having pale
patch in forewing cell very small
or absent: two submarginal
spots on forewing. Sexes alike.
Range and Habitat An uncommon forest species found
in the Cameroons, West Africa.

GRAPHIUM ALMANSOR Hourath
Identification Wingspan 6½–8
cm. A small tailless swallowtail, dark brown with pale
ochreous markings not ar-
ranged in the form of a band as
in related species: with or without submarginal pale spots:
sexes similar.
Range and Habitat An uncommon and local forest swallowtail found in West Africa,
eastwards through the Congo

to southern Sudan, Ethiopia, Uganda, north-western Tanzania and western
Kenya. Flies throughout the year.

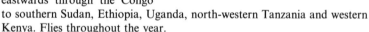

GRAPHIUM ODIN Strand
Identification Wingspan 6½–7½
cm. A small tailless swallowtail, blackish with white markings, including small patch in
forewing cell: subapical patch
small. Sexes alike.
Range and Habitat An uncommon forest swallowtail
found in the Cameroons and
the Congo.

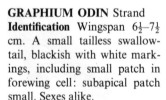

GRAPHIUM OLBRECHTSI
Berger
Identification Wingspan 6½–7 cm. ♂ a small, tailless swallowtail, pale warm brown with light ochreous-yellow markings. Closely related to *Graphium odin*. ♀ unknown.

Range and Habitat A very rare species known only from a few specimens from Sankuru, Lomami River and Lualaba, Congo.

GRAPHIUM AURIVILLIUSI
Seeldrayers
Identification Wingspan 7½cm. ♂ a small tailless swallowtail, blackish-brown with green-tinged white markings: three parallel elongated spots in forewing cell: extensive submarginal spotting on hindwing. ♀ unknown.

Range and Habitat Known only from the type specimen from the Congo: precise locality not known.

GRAPHIUM AGAMEDES
Westwood
Identification Wingspan 5½–6½cm. A small tailless swallowtail, blackish-brown with white markings: apex of forewing lightly scaled and semi-transparent: submarginal spots in forewing small and ill-defined or absent. Sexes alike.

Range and Habitat An uncommon and local forest species found in Ghana and the northern Congo forests.

PAPILIONIDAE – SWALLOWTAILS

1 **GRAPHIUM GUDENUSI** ♂   *page* 68
Sexes similar: straight green median band.

2 **GRAPHIUM NIGRESCENS** ♂   69
Sexes similar: green stripes on forewing very narrow and broken.

3 **GRAPHIUM JUNODI** ♂   70
Sexes similar: markings cream: two broad bands on hindwing.

4 **GRAPHIUM ILLYRIS** ♂   67
Sexes similar: straight yellow median band.

5 **GRAPHIUM ANTHEUS** ♂   71
Sexes similar: green forewing bars curved: tails relatively short.

6 **GRAPHIUM POLICENES** ♂   70
Sexes similar: green forewing bars straight: red spot at tornus of
hindwing.

7 **GRAPHIUM COLONNA** ♂   68
Sexes similar: black with narrow greenish-blue markings: two red
spots near tornus of hindwing.

8 **GRAPHIUM KIRBYI** ♂   67
Sexes similar: narrow straight whitish median band.

9 **GRAPHIUM TYNDERAEUS** ♂   59
Sexes similar: green submarginal spots present.

10 **GRAPHIUM UCALEGON** ♂   60
Sexes similar: pale ochreous median band.

11 **GRAPHIUM POLISTRATUS** ♂   69
Sexes similar: no red spots at tornus of hindwing.

12 **GRAPHIUM PORTHAON** ♂   71
Sexes similar: light markings cream or greenish-cream.

13 **GRAPHIUM LATREILLIANUS** ♂   59
♂ no green submarginal spots on forewing: ♀ resembles ♂ but with pale
cream not green markings.

14 **GRAPHIUM RIDLEYANUS** ♂   58
Sexes similar, but ♀ has rounder wings: some examples greyish-brown
not red.

15 **GRAPHIUM PHILONOE** ♂   68
Sexes similar: differs from related species in lacking ochreous and red
markings on underside.

16 **GRAPHIUM LEONIDAS** ♂   66
Sexes similar: rounded pale blue markings.

PLATE 6   65

PIERIDAE – WHITES

1   **EUREMA HECABE** ♂   *page* 98
     Sexes similar: bright yellow: black border of forewing angled inwards
     below apex.

2   **EUREMA HAPALE** ♂   99
     Sexes similar: very pale yellow: restricted black apical patch on
     forewing.

3   **EUREMA BRIGITTA** ♂♂   98
     Sexes similar: wings often dusky yellow: broad black margins.

4   **EUREMA DESJARDINSI** ♂♀   99
     Sexes similar: hindwing distinctly angled.

5   **MYLOTHRIS POPPEA** ♂♀   82
     ♂ orange patch at base forewing: ♀ more extensive orange basal patch.

6   **MYLOTHRIS SAGALA** ♂♀   83
     Sexes similar: forewing with varying amount of black: hindwing
     mainly yellow.

7   **BELENOIS RAFFRAYI** ♂   76
     Sexes similar: hindwing black and pale grey.

8   **MYLOTHRIS CHLORIS** ♂♀   79
     ♂ orange basal patch on underside forewing: ♀ yellowish to orange.

9   **BELENOIS THYSA** ♂ ♂u ♀   77
     No black bar at end of cell of forewing.

10 **NEPHERONIA ARGIA** ♂♀♀♀   95
     ♂ white to pale bluish-white: underside without silky sheen: ♀ variable,
     with or without red basal patch.

11 **NEPHERONIA THALASSINA** ♂♀   94
     ♂ distinctly bluish-white: underside with silky sheen: ♀ hindwings white
     or yellowish.

12 **COLIAS ELECTO** ♂♀♀   95
     Orange forewings with black border, spotted yellow in ♀: less common
     form of ♀ has forewings greenish-white, not orange.

13 **ERONIA LEDA** ♂♀♀   94
     ♂ bright yellow with orange tip: ♀ paler, with or without orange tip.

14 **ERONIA CLEODORA** ♂ ♂u   93
     Sexes similar: creamy-white with wide black border.

GRAPHIUM ADAMASTOR Boisduval
Identification Wingspan 5½–7½cm. A small tailless swallowtail, blackish-brown with white markings. Closely related to *Graphium agamedes* from which it may be distinguished by having the white patch in the forewing cell very large and completely bisecting the cell.

Range and Habitat West African forests from Ghana to Dahomey: an uncommon and local butterfly.

GRAPHIUM PHILONOE Ward   p 64
White-dappled Swallowtail
Identification Wingspan 6–7½cm. A tailless swallowtail with white markings. Sexes alike. May be distinguished from the somewhat similar *Graphium pylades* and *Graphium taboranus* by absence of red and ochreous markings on underside of wings.
Range and Habitat Inhabits coastal bush, wooded areas and light forest. Common in coastal areas of Kenya and Tanzania: also occurs in southern Sudan, northern Uganda and south-western Ethiopia. Flight relatively weak: easily captured. On the wing throughout the year.

Larval Food Plants Various species of *Anona* (Anonaceae).

GRAPHIUM LEONIDAS Fabricius   p 64
Veined Swallowtail
Identification Wingspan 7–8cm. A tailless swallowtail, black with pale blue semi-translucent markings. Mimics *Danaus limniace* (Danaidae) both in its colour and its sailing flight. Sexes alike, but some specimens with less extensive blue markings.
Range and Habitat A common species throughout Africa except in desert areas and high mountains. Most frequent in bush and lightly wooded areas and forest

outskirts. In South Africa flies from September to April: in more tropical countries on the wing throughout the year.

Larval Food Plants Various members of the family Anonaceae, including cultivated Custard Apple.

GRAPHIUM KIRBYI Hewitson

Kirby's Swordtail

Identification Wingspan 5½–7cm. This species and the swallowtails which follow are known as Swordtails on account of their long, straight, slender tails. A blackish or greyish-brown swordtail with a straight, narrow white or greenish-white median band: pale grey submarginal crescents on hindwing. Sexes alike.

Range and Habitat A local but sometimes common species in coastal scrub, woodland and forest in eastern Kenya and Tanzania. Also reputed to occur in Nigeria, but record may be due to misidentification. Flight relatively weak and fluttering; much attracted to flowering shrubs and ♂♂ often drink on damp sand. ♀ relatively rare. On the wing throughout the year but commonest during and after rains.

Larval Food Plants *Anona* (Anonaceae).

GRAPHIUM ILLYRIS Hewitson

Yellow-banded Swordtail

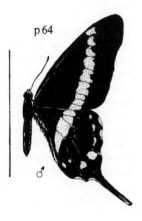

Identification Wingspan 7–9cm. A dark brown swordtail with a relatively narrow yellow median band and yellow submarginal spots on the hindwing. Sexes alike, but ♀ usually larger, with larger submarginal spots on hindwing.

Range and Habitat A forest species found in West Africa and the Congo.

GRAPHIUM GUDENUSI Rebel   p 64
Kigezi Swordtail

Identification Wingspan 7–8cm. A black swordtail with a deeply serrated hindwing and a straight green median band; green submarginal spots on fore and hindwings; sexes similar.

Range and Habitat A rare and very local swordtail confined to mountain forests of Kigezi, south-western Uganda, and adjacent highland areas of Kivu, eastern Congo, and Rwanda and Burundi. ♂♂ have habit of following rivers and streams through forest, sometimes settling on sand bars to drink. Flies throughout the year.

GRAPHIUM COLONNA Ward   p 64
Mamba Swordtail

Identification Wingspan 6½–8cm. A velvety-black swordtail with narrow greenish-blue markings; centre of hindwing black, unmarked; two conspicuous red spots near tornus of hindwing: sexes similar but ♀ is usually larger. The similar *Graphium polistratus* has extra greenish-blue markings on hindwing but lacks red spots.

Range and Habitat Coastal and near coastal areas of Kenya and Tanzania, south through Mozambique to Natal, South Africa. Inhabits coastal forests and woodland, and also dense coastal scrub. ♂♂ much attracted to damp places along forest roads. ♀♀ much rarer than

♂♂, usually seen feeding at flowering shrubs in early morning. Flies from late September to early April in South Africa; further north on the wing throughout the year but most numerous during the rainy seasons.

Larval Food Plants *Artabotrys* (Anonaceae).

GRAPHIUM POLISTRATUS Grose-Smith
Dancing Swordtail

Identification Wingspan $6\frac{1}{2}$–$7\frac{1}{2}$ cm. A black swordtail with green stripes and spots more extensive than in *Graphium colonna*, from which it also differs in lacking red spots near the tornus of the hindwing. Sexes alike but ♀ tends to be larger.

Range and Habitat Inhabits open forests and woodland and coastal scrub from eastern Kenya, south through Tanzania, Malawi and Mozambique to northern Natal, South Africa. In south on wing from September to May: further north flies throughout the year.

p 64

p 64

GRAPHIUM NIGRESCENS Eimer
Dusky Swordtail

Identification Wingspan 6–$7\frac{1}{2}$ cm. A black swordtail with green markings, distinguished from related species in having the streaks from the forewing costal margin very narrow and broken. Usually lacks red spot at tornus of hindwing. Sexes alike.

Range and Habitat This is a rare forest swordtail recorded from the Cameroons and the Congo. The ♀ is seldom encountered and is very rare in collections. Flies throughout the year.

GRAPHIUM POLICENES Cramer

p 64

Small Striped Swordtail

Identification Wingspan 7–7½cm. A black swordtail with pale, bright green markings and a red spot at tornus of hindwing: green bars from forewing costal margin straight. Sexes alike. *Graphium polistratus* has no red spot on hindwing: *Graphium antheus* has curved green forewing bars.

Range and Habitat A widely distributed species found in forests and woodland from West Africa and the Sudan to Natal and northern Cape Province, South Africa. On the wing from late August to April in South Africa: throughout the year further north.

Larval Food Plants *Uraria caffra* and *Artabotrys* (Anonaceae).

GRAPHIUM JUNODI Trimen

p 64

Mozambique Swordtail

Identification Wingspan 8–8½cm. A blackish-brown swordtail with heavy cream or slightly greenish-cream markings: two broad pale bands on hindwing: no red spot near tornus of hindwing. Sexes similar. *Graphium porthaon* is also black and cream, but markings are quite different.

Range and Habitat A rare swordtail confined to forests of Mozambique and the eastern border of Rhodesia (eastern side of Vumba Mts.). It is perhaps most frequent in the Dondo forest, near Beira, Mozambique. Flies mainly from August to May.

GRAPHIUM ANTHEUS Cramer
Large Striped Swordtail

p 64

Identification Wingspan 8–10½cm. A large blackish swordtail with bright green markings: green bars from forewing costal margin heavy and S-shaped: two red spots at tornus of hindwing: tail rather shorter than in related species and slightly curved. Sexes alike but ♀ usually larger.

Range and Habitat A common species throughout most of the African continent south to Natal, South Africa. Inhabits forested regions, woodland, savannah and bush country. Flies throughout the year except in south, when on the wing from August to April. A swift flier but ♂♂ often congregate on damp mud: ♀♀ much less common.

Larval Food Plants Several members of the Anonaceae family, including *Artabotrys*, *Uvaria caffra* and various cultivated Custard apples (*Anona*).

GRAPHIUM PORTHAON Hewitson
Cream-striped Swordtail

p 64

Identification Wingspan 8–9cm. A blackish-brown swordtail with creamy-white markings: creamy-white bars from forewing costal margin narrow and S-shaped. Sexes similar. *Graphium antheus* also has S-shaped costal bars, but these are heavier and bright green, not cream.

Range and Habitat Found in wooded country, savannah and coastal bush from eastern Kenya south through Tanzania, Malawi, Mozambique and Rhodesia to northern Transvaal and northern Natal, South Africa. In south flies from August to April, elsewhere throughout the year.

Larval Food Plants *Artabotrys* (Anonaceae).

FAMILY PIERIDAE
WHITES

The Whites are a group of medium-sized butterflies, usually with a white or yellow basic colour; often with coloured or black tips to the forewings. Characters of the Family include front legs well-developed in both sexes with claws bifid or toothed; cells in both fore and hindwings closed distally, as in Papilionidae, but two anal veins present in hindwing. Many species are strong fliers and some, such as *Catopsilia florella*, have migratory habits: other species are feeble fliers, frequently settling on the ground or on flowers. In tropical areas many species produce three, four, or even more broods during the year and many exhibit strong seasonal dimorphism. 'Wet season' forms are larger and show heavier pigmentation, whilst extreme 'dry season' broods are small with greatly reduced dark markings.

Early Stages. The eggs are elongate with longitudinal ribs, generally white or yellowish: these are laid singly or in clusters on or near the food plant. The larvae are cylindrical, usually green, with a coating of soft short fine hairs. Many feed on families Capparidaceae and Cruciferae. The pupae have a dorsal keel, and a single anterior projection at the head; they are attached by the tail and supported by a silken girdle.

PSEUDOPONTIA PARADOXA Plotz
Moth-like White

Identification Wingspan 3–3½cm. Sexes alike. A delicate, round-winged completely white butterfly, resembling a small *Leptosia* without markings. Antennae and wing venation remarkable, the former without a defined terminal club.

Range and Habitat Forests of West Africa, the Congo and western Uganda, where most frequent in Kalinzu Forest. Slow weak flight in shade, often amongst forest undergrowth.

4cm

APPIAS SYLVIA Fabricius
Woodland White

Identification Wingspan 5½–6cm. ♂ white above and below, with basal area of forewing suffused with orange: margins of wings with small spots: ♀ resembles ♂ but forewing yellowish, and orange basal area usually wider. Resembles some ♀ forms of *Appias sabina* but

has more rounded forewing. This species is a remarkable mimic of *Mylothris rhodope* ♂, from which it may be distinguished by presence of a tuft of hairs (corema) at the end of the abdomen on the underside, just in front of the genitalia, and by more numerous marginal spots on hindwing.

Range and Habitat Forests and well wooded areas of West Africa, Congo, Uganda, the Sudan, Ethiopia, Kenya, southwards to Tanzania, Malawi and Rhodesia.

APPIAS PHAOLA Doubleday
Congo White

Identification Wingspan 5½–6cm. ♂ white; forewing with black costal margin and broad black marginal band: hindwing with round black marginal spots. ♀ greyish-white: forewing suffused blackish at base; black apex and marginal band spotted yellowish white; hindwing

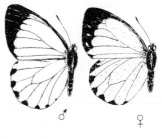

whitish or yellowish with heavy black marginal spots.

Range and Habitat A forest species found in West Africa, the Congo, Uganda and western Tanzania.

APPIAS LASTI Grose-Smith

Identification Wingspan 5cm. ♂ forewing white with a black apex: hindwing sulphur yellow with small black marginal spots. ♀ similar but black apex and marginal spots larger. Species resembles *Mylothris trimenia* but distin-

guished by tuft of hairs (corema) at tip of abdomen below, in front of genitalia.
Range and Habitat Forest areas and wooded country Kenya and Tanzania.
Uncommon.

APPIAS SABINA Felder

Identification Wingspan 4½–5cm. ♂
white above with blackish triangular spots at apex and along
margin of forewing; hindwing
with small round marginal dots:
underside white with upper edge of
hindwing narrowly edged orange.
♀ yellowish-white with dull orange
patch at base of forewing: in some
specimens hindwing distinctly pale
yellow: black markings more extensive than in ♂.

Range and Habitat Mainly a forest
and woodland insect, found in
West Africa, the Congo, to Uganda and Kenya, south through Tanzania to
eastern border of Rhodesia. Flies throughout the year.

APPIAS EPAPHIA Cramer
Diverse White

Identification Wingspan 5½–6cm. ♂
white with black apical patch, continued as spots along part of forewing margin but no spot on vein
at bottom; underside of forewing
bright yellow at base. ♀ white with
very heavy black markings: in
some specimens white replaced by
pale yellow.

Range and Habitat A widespread
species over much of Africa and
also in Madagascar. Occurs in for-
rested and wooded areas and in
more open bush country. In South

Africa on the wing from March to July; throughout the year elsewhere.
Larval Food Plants *Capparis*, *Boscia* and *Niebuhria*.

BELENOIS GIDICA Godart
African Veined White
Identification Wingspan 5–6½cm. A
fairly large white with apex of forewing acute. ♂ white with brownish-
black markings. ♀ whitish or
yellowish with very broad brown
marginal bands on both wings:
forewing suffused with brown at
base and large blackish spot in cell.
Dry season forms are paler than
wet season examples with reduced
dark markings.

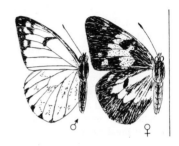

Range and Habitat A common
species in West, Central and East
Africa, south to South Africa:
mainly an insect of wooded areas
and tall scrub. A swift flier but
much attracted to low-growing
flowering plants and bushes.
Larval Food Plants Various species of *Capparis*.

BELENOIS CREONA Cramer
African Common White
Identification Wingspan 5–6cm. ♂
a medium-sized white with broad
black border to both wings and
small white spots in the border:
small black dot in cell of forewing.
♀ has basal two-thirds of wings
cream or yellowish with a pearly
lustre, the outer third dark brown,
with or without pale spots: small
dark spot at end of cell.

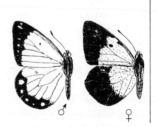

Range and Habitat Widespread and
abundant throughout most of
Africa, in wooded areas, savannah
bush and scrub and open country.
Species sometimes migratory. Flight strong but much attracted to low-growing
flowers and shrubs. Flies throughout the year.
Larval Food Plants Various species of *Capparis*.

BELENOIS AUROTA Fabricius
Brown-veined White

Identification Wingspan 4–6cm. ♂ white, with white-spotted dark brown marginal borders and curved wedge-shaped patch in the cell of forewing. ♀ white or creamy-yellow with brown margins; broad and curved wedge-shaped patch in cell of forewing. ♂ similar to *Belenois zochalia* but lacks two

longitudinal dark lines in cell on underside of hindwing.

Range and Habitat Found through-out Africa and abundant in many habitats from forest edges, woodland and savannah to semi-desert bush. Flies throughout the year.

Larval Food Plants Various species of *Capparis* and Caper tree, *Boscia*.

BELENOIS RAFFRAYI Oberthur

p 65

Raffray's White

Identification Wingspan 5–5½cm. A very distinct species; forewings black with a bluish-white basal patch; hindwings black, merging to blue-grey in basal third. Sexes similar but ♀ usually slightly larger with slightly rounder wings. Differs from all other species in having underside of hindwing uniform black.

Range and Habitat A mountain forest species found in highlands of Ethiopia, Kenya, Uganda,

Tanzania and the eastern Congo. On the wing throughout the year.

BELENOIS ZOCHALIA Boisduval
Forest White

Identification Wingspan 5½–6½ cm. ♂ white with blackish apex containing five white spots: curved black patch in forewing cell: hindwing with triangular black marginal spots more or less developed. ♀ resembles ♂ but is cream or yellowish-white with slight pearly sheen. Under-

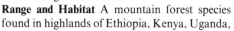

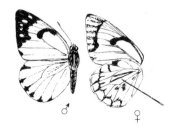

side of hindwing in both sexes has two longitudinal brown lines in cell, which distinguish this species from similar *Belenois aurota*.

Range and Habitat An eastern species ranging from Ethiopia, Uganda and Kenya southwards to South Africa. Inhabits forested and wooded areas. Flies from September to June in South Africa; throughout the year further north.

Larval Food Plants *Maerua* (Capparidaceae).

BELENOIS CALYPSO Drury

Identification Wingspan 5½–6½cm. ♂ white to creamy-white with white-spotted black apical patch, continued as narrow toothed marginal band; hindwing white with triangular marginal spots; underside with large black spot at end of hindwing cell. ♀ suffused blackish at base of forewing: broad black apical patch: marginal bands without distinct whitish spots.

Range and Habitat West Africa, the Congo to Uganda and Tanzania: inhabits forested and wooded areas. Flies throughout the year.

BELENOIS THYSA Hopffer
False Dotted Border

p 65

Identification Wingspan 6–7½cm. ♂ white with triangular black marginal spots and black sub-marginal dots: no black patch in forewing cell; underside of hindwing orange, which shows faintly through on upperside. ♀ resembles ♂ in pattern but ochreous-orange, not white.

Range and Habitat A forest and woodland butterfly ranging from Somalia and Ethiopia south to South Africa, west to Angola and the Congo. Flies throughout the year except in extreme south where on the wing from September to April.

BELENOIS SOLILUCIS Butler

Identification Wingspan 6–7cm. ♂ bright sulphur-yellow with black apical patch and rounded black marginal spots. ♀ paler, yellowish-white; forewing with triangular black marginal spots; hindwing with rounded black marginal spots.

Range and Habitat Forests and wooded areas; West Africa from Cameroons and Angola to the Congo and Uganda; sometimes very abundant along forest roads. Flies throughout the year.

DIXEIA PIGEA Boisduval
Anthill White

Identification Wingspan 4½–6cm. ♂ a small all-white butterfly with very reduced or no dark markings on apex and margin of forewing. Very similar to dry season forms of *Dixeia doxo*, but may be distinguished by its much shorter antennae. ♀ variable: white with yellow hindwings; all wings ochreous yellow; or all wings white with ochreous patch at base of forewings.

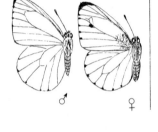

Range and Habitat A species of forested areas and woodland found in the southern Sudan and Kenya, south to South Africa, west to Angola and the Cameroons. Flies throughout the year. Much attracted to low-growing flowering plants and flowering bushes.

Larval Food Plants Various species of *Capparis*.

DIXEIA SPILLERI Spiller
Spiller's Yellow

Identification Wingspan 4–4½cm. ♂ a small sulphur-yellow species with restricted black markings on apex and upper margin of forewing. ♀ resembles ♂ but usually the yellow is slightly duller.

Range and Habitat A woodland and forest butterfly found in coastal districts of Kenya, south to Natal, South Africa. In South Africa flies from September to June: throughout the year further north.

DIXEIA DOXO Godart
African Small White

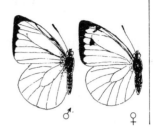

Identification Wingspan 4–5cm. ♂ a small white with a black tip on apex, sometimes with veins on fore and hindwings darkened. ♀ has a more extensive black apex and marginal markings, and a larger round submarginal spot on forewings. Dry season form of ♂ very similar to *Dixeia pigea* but always distinguished by longer antennae.

Range and Habitat Widely distributed throughout Ethiopian Region, but local and range not continuous. Inhabits open forest, savannah woodlands and bush country. Flies throughout the year.

Larval Food Plants Various species of *Capparis*.

MYLOTHRIS TRIMENIA Butler
Trimen's Dotted Border

Identification Wingspan 5–6½cm. ♂ forewing white with a black apex and round black marginal spots: hindwing lemon yellow with round black marginal spots. ♀ resembles ♂ but hindwing ochreous yellow and marginal spots usually larger.

Range and Habitat A forest and woodland butterfly found in South Africa where it occurs in Natal, Eastern Cape Province and Transvaal. Flight characteristic of the Mylothris whites, relatively slow and buoyant, often high up amongst foliage of trees. Flies throughout the year.

Larval Food Plants Various species of parasitic *Loranthus*.

MYLOTHRIS CHLORIS Fabricius   p 65
Dotted Border

Identification Wingspan 5–7½cm. ♂ white with black apical patch and black marginal spots: very faint pinkish tinge at base of forewing: ♀ similar in pattern but pinkish-orange or orange-yellow, not white.

Range and Habitat Widely distributed in tropical and southern Africa. Inhabits forests, woodland and bush country. Typical *Mylothris*

PIERIDAE – WHITES

1 **PINACOPTERYX ERIPHIA** ♂   *page* 84
   Sexes similar.

2 **COLOTIS CALAIS** ♂   85
   Sexes similar: orange basal patch.

3 **COLOTIS AURIGINEUS** ♂   85
   Sexes similar.

4 **COLOTIS VESTA** ♂   86
   Sexes similar.

5 **COLOTIS ERONE** ♂♀   87
   ♂ three violet spots in black apical patch: ♀ variable, one form with
   white spotted black apical patch.

6 **COLOTIS CELIMENE** ♂ ♂u ♀   86
   ♂ crimson streaks in apical patch.

7 **COLOTIS HALIMEDE** ♂ ♀ws ♀ds   87
   Orange-yellow patches less developed in dry season form.

8 **COLOTIS IONE** ♂ ♀♀♀♀   87
   Usually 4 or 5 violet spots in apical patch: ♀ very variable.

9 **COLOTIS REGINA** ♂♀   88
   ♂ large, broad violet apical patch: ♀ white or yellowish.

10 **COLOTIS HETAERA** ♂ ♀♀   88
   ♂ with more than three crimson apical spots: ♀ yellow or cream.

11 **COLOTIS EUNOMA** ♂♂ ♀   88
   ♂ three crimson apical spots.

12 **COLOTIS HILDEBRANDTI** ♂ ♀   89
   ♂ orange-gold apical patch.

13 **COLOTIS ELGONENSIS** ♂   89
   ♀ without red apical spots.

14 **COLOTIS DANAE** ♂ ♂u ♀ds ♀ws   90
   Brown spots on underside of hindwing.

1 2 3 4 5 ♂ 5 ♀

6 ♂ 6 ♂ u 6 ♀ 7 ♂ 7 ♀ 7 ♀ ds

8 ♂ 8 ♀ 8 ♀ 8 ♀ 8 ♀

9 ♂ 9 ♀ 10 ♂ 10 ♀ 10 ♀

11 ♀ 11 ♂ 11 ♀ 12 ♂ 12 ♀

13 14 ♂ 14 u 14 ♀ 14 ♀

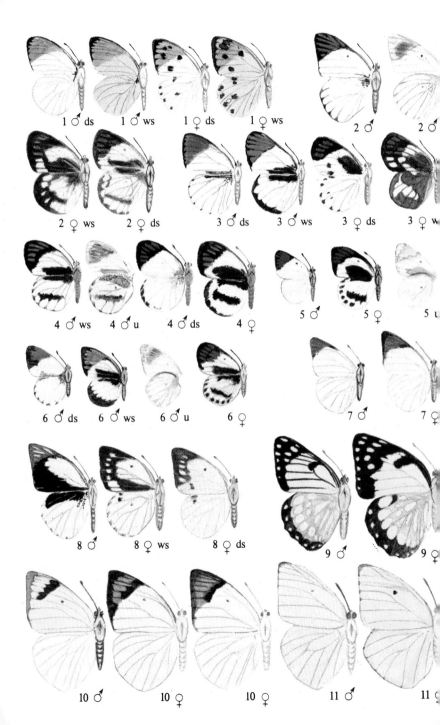

1 ♂ ds   1 ♂ ws   1 ♀ ds   1 ♀ ws   2 ♂   2 ♂

2 ♀ ws   2 ♀ ds   3 ♂ ds   3 ♂ ws   3 ♀ ds   3 ♀ w

4 ♂ ws   4 ♂ u   4 ♂ ds   4 ♀   5 ♂   5 ♀   5 u

6 ♂ ds   6 ♂ ws   6 ♂ u   6 ♀   7 ♂   7 ♀

8 ♂   8 ♀ ws   8 ♀ ds   9 ♂   9 ♀

10 ♂   10 ♀   10 ♀   11 ♂   11 ♀

PLATE 8   81

PIERIDAE – WHITES

1   **COLOTIS EUCHARIS** ♂ds ♂ws ♀ds ♀ws   90
White in dry season forms, yellow in wet season forms.

2   **COLOTIS ANTEVIPPE** ♂ ♂u ♀ws ♀ds   90
♂ straight inner edge to red apical patch: veins darkened on underside.

3   **COLOTIS EVENINA** ♂ds ♂ws ♀ds ♀ws   91
Orange apical patch in ♂: ♀, black forewing bar slants upwards.

4   **COLOTIS EUIPPE** ♂ws ♂u ♂ds ♀   91
Forewing rounded: red apical patch curved.

5   **COLOTIS PALLENE** ♂ ♀ u   92
Underside, apical patch yellow.

6   **COLOTIS EVAGORE** ♂ds ♂ws ♂u ♀   92
♂ orange-red apical patch with black notch on inner edge: ♀ white or
yellowish: apical spots variable, red or whitish.

7   **COLOTIS AGOYE** ♂ ♀   92
Forewing apex pointed.

8   **COLOTIS ERIS** ♂ ♀   93

9   **COLOTIS PROTOMEDIA** ♂ ♀   86

10 **COLOTIS SUBFASCIATUS** ♂ ♀ ♀   93

11 **CATOPSILIA FLORELLA** ♂ ♀   98

flight, slow and buoyant, often high. Flies throughout the year.
Larval Food Plants Various species of parasitic *Loranthus*.

MYLOTHRIS POPPEA Cramer   p 65
Twin Dotted Border

Identification Wingspan 5½–6½cm. ♂ white
with black apical patch and small black marginal dots, sometimes absent on hindwing:
bright orange-red patch on base of forewing,
continued as a yellow suffusion on base of hindwing. ♀ similar but reddish forewing patch more
extensive and larger black marginal dots.
Range and Habitat Widely distributed in forest
and wooded areas throughout Ethiopian
Region. Flight slow and buoyant, often high
amongst foliage of trees. On wing throughout the year.
Larval Food Plants Various species of parasitic *Loranthus*.

♂   4cm

MYLOTHRIS YULEI Butler
Yule's Dotted Border

Identification Wingspan 4½–5½cm. ♂ creamy-
white with black apical patch; black marginal ˙
dots small; bar of forewing suffused orange-
yellow; ♀ similar to ♂ but with more extensive
suffusion of orange-yellow at base of both fore
and hindwings: marginal dots larger.
Range and Habitat Occurs in forested and
wooded areas from Ethiopia, Kenya and
Uganda south to Mozambique, Rhodesia and
southern Congo: an isolated population in the
Cameroons, West Africa. Flies throughout the
year.

♂

MYLOTHRIS RHODOPE Fabricius
Tropical Dotted Border

Identification Wingspan 5½–6cm. ♂ white with
an extensive black apical patch and six round
black marginal spots on hindwing: rather small,
oblique orange-yellow patch at base of forewing. ♀ variable, forewing white or suffused
yellowish; apical patch broken up into series

♂

of elongated vein streaks. ♂ similar to *Appias sylvia* but has only six marginal spots on hindwing.
Range and Habitat A West African forest species extending to Uganda and western Kenya, south to southern Congo. Flies throughout the year.

MYLOTHRIS SAGALA Grose-Smith   p 65
Dusky Dotted Border

Identification Wingspan 5–5½cm. ♂ forewing dusky brown with variable whitish central area; hindwing lemon yellow with marginal dark patch followed by marginal dots. ♀ similar but marginal hindwing patch and spots less extensive.
Range and Habitat A forest insect, widespread in tropical Africa and East Africa, south to Malawi and eastern Rhodesia. Flies throughout the year.
Larval Food Plants Various species of *Loranthus*.

♂

MYLOTHRIS BERNICE Hewitson
Swamp Dotted Border

Identification Wingspan 4½–5cm. ♂ creamy-white with narrow apical black patch and small black marginal dots on fore and hindwings: orange-red stripe at base of costa; costa edged blackish. ♀ similar to ♂ but usually more yellowish and sometimes wings tinged greyish.
Range and Habitat Ranges from the Cameroons to the Congo, Uganda and Kenya, south to Malawi and Rhodesia at Victoria Falls. Occurs mainly in and around swamps and marshes.

♂   4cm

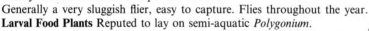

Generally a very sluggish flier, easy to capture. Flies throughout the year.
Larval Food Plants Reputed to lay on semi-aquatic *Polygonium*.

LEPTOSIA MEDUSA Cramer
Congo Wood White
Identification Wingspan 4½–5½cm. A fragile round-winged species. Both sexes white with black apical band and large round spot below apex; hindwing with or without very narrow black marginal band.

♂

Range and Habitat A forest species found in West Africa, the Congo, Uganda, western Tanzania and Kenya. A weak flier with a fluttering flight, keeping to forest shade. On wing throughout the year.

LEPTOSIA ALCESTA Cramer
African Wood White

Identification Wingspan $3\frac{1}{2}$–$4\frac{1}{2}$cm. Small fragile white butterfly with rounded wings: markings variable, usually a black apical patch and a black spot on forewing; in some examples apical patch much reduced and black spot absent. Sexes alike.

♂   4cm

Range and Habitat West Africa, the Congo, Uganda and Kenya, southwards to Rhodesia and South Africa. Inhabits forests and dense woodland. Flight weak and buoyant: keeps to shade inside forest, flying within a few feet of the ground. On the wing throughout the year.

Larval Food Plants *Richiea.*

PONTIA HELICE Linnaeus
. Meadow White

Identification Wingspan 4–5cm. ♂ white with a black apical patch with white spots: curved black patch in forewing cell: hindwing margined black: ♀ has more extensive black margin to hindwing and submarginal spot in forewing. Underside forewings white with greenish apical markings; hindwings with veins broadly edged greenish and gold. Easily distinguished from similar species by pattern of underside markings.

♂   ♂u   4cm

Range and Habitat A common species in open bush country and grasslands, Ethiopian Region, but distribution not continuous. Flies throughout the year.

Larval Food Plants *Reseda pruniosa.*

PINACOPTERYX ERIPHIA Godart   p 80
Zebra White

Identification Wingspan $5\frac{1}{2}$–$6\frac{1}{2}$cm. ♂ a dark brown or buffish-brown white

with pale or deep yellow bands and spots. ♀
similar to ♂ but often larger and pale markings
sometimes less well defined. Dry season forms
are paler than those of wet season.

p 80

Range and Habitat Widely distributed in open
bush country and grasslands with bush over
Ethiopian Region, from Somalia and Ethiopia
to South Africa, and in Angola. Relatively weak
flier, much attracted to low-growing flowering
plants. Flies throughout the year.

♂

Larval Food Plants *Capparis oleoides*, and *Maerua triphylla*.

COLOTIS CALAIS Cramer

p 80

Topaz Arab

Identification Wingspan 3½–4½cm. Pinkish-orange, paler
and more yellowish on hindwing, with extensive black or
dark brown markings; large black patch in forewing cell:
hindwing without distinct dark discal band which is
present in closely related *Colotis vesta*; veins of wings
not darkened. Sexes similar, but ♀ usually paler.

Range and Habitat Widely distributed throughout most
of the Ethiopian Region, outside forest areas, south to
northern Transvaal, South Africa. It inhabits open dry
savannah country and arid bush country. Its flight is low

♂   4cm

and not very strong: much attracted to flowering plants and bushes. On the
wing throughout the year.

Larval Food Plants *Salvadora persica*.

COLOTIS AURIGINEUS Butler

p 80

Double-banded Orange

Identification Wingspan 4½–5cm. Deep orange
with black markings: veins black and black
patch in cell: extreme base fore and hindwings
bluish-grey; black discal band on fore and
hindwings. Sexes similar but ♀ sometimes paler.

Range and Habitat An open bush and dry
country species found in southern Sudan,
northern Uganda, Ethiopia and Somalia to
Kenya, Tanzania and Malawi. A common
insect in the dry bush country of eastern Kenya.
Flies throughout the year.

♂   4cm

COLOTIS VESTA Reiche   p 80
Veined Orange

Identification Wingspan 4½–6cm. Basal half of wings white, sometimes greyish; washed pinkish-orange towards marginal band: outer half black or dark brown with large pale orange or cream spots, in the hindwing forming marginal and discal bands. Sexes similar but ♀ paler.

Range and Habitat Widely distributed throughout Ethiopian Region in suitable areas from Ethiopia south to northern Transvaal and northern Natal, South Africa. Found in dry savannah and bush country. Flies throughout the year.

♂   4cm

COLOTIS PROTOMEDIA Klug   p 81
Veined Yellow

Identification Wingspan 5–6½cm. A large, bright yellow species with blackish-brown apex and marginal bands spotted with yellow: curved black patch in cell. Sexes similar but ♂ has veins of forewing black: ♀ lacks black forewing veins and is larger.

Range and Habitat A desert scrub or arid bush country species found in West Africa (northern Nigeria) to Sudan, Ethiopia and Somalia, south to Uganda, Kenya and Tanzania. Flies throughout the year.

♂

COLOTIS CELIMENE Lucas   p 80
Lilac Tip

Identification Wingspan 4–4½cm. ♂ creamy-white with apical area black containing crimson streaks; hindwing with blackish marginal band: ♀ has white-spotted black apical patch: underside sulphur yellow to white with chequered pattern on hindwing.

Range and Habitat Inhabits open savannah and dry bush country from Ethiopia southwards through Uganda, Kenya and Tanzania to Transvaal, South Africa and South-West Africa. Flight rapid. On the wing throughout the year.

♂   4cm

COLOTIS HALIMEDE Klug
p 80
Orange Patch White

Identification Wingspan 4½–5½cm. ♂ white with pale grey basal patches, a grey costa and apex and grey marginal spots: orange patches on fore and hindwings and curved row of grey spots on hindwing. ♀ has reduced orange patches, sometimes absent in dry season forms, and a band of grey spots on forewing.

Range and Habitat Inhabits open bush and semi-desert bush country from West Africa (Senegal) eastwards to Sudan, Ethiopia and Somalia, south through Kenya to Tanzania. Flight rapid, but often settles on the ground.

COLOTIS ERONE Angas
p 80
Coast Purple Tip

Identification Wingspan 5–6½cm. ♂ white, sometimes with darkened veins; black apical patch enclosing three violet spots. ♀ variable, apical patch may enclose red or white spots. *Colotis ione* ♂ has four or five violet spots in apical patch, and *Colotis regina* has a large broad violet patch.

Range and Habitat Distribution rather restricted, found along the east coast of South Africa, the Transvaal, to South-West Africa, north to Zambia. Inhabits bush country, open woodland and coastal areas: flight rapid and active.

Larval Food Plants *Niebuhria pedunculosa* (Capparidaceae).

4cm

COLOTIS IONE Godart
p 80
Purple Tip

Identification Wingspan 5½–7cm. ♂ white, with or without blackened veins: black apical patch enclosing five to six purple spots. ♀ extremely variable (see plate 7), white with apical patch black with red spots, black with white spots or red with reduced black margins. *Colotis erone* ♂ has only three purple spots in apical patch: *Colotis regina* ♂ has large, broad violet apical patch edged and veined with black.

Range and Habitat Widely distributed in Ethiopian Region, south to South-West Africa, and Natal and Transvaal, South Africa. Inhabits bush country, savannah and open woodland. Strong flier. On the wing throughout the year.
Larval Food Plants Various species of Family Capparidaceae.

COLOTIS REGINA Trimen   p 80
Regal Purple Tip

Identification Wingspan 6½–7½cm. ♂ white, with or without darkened veins; large broad purple apical patch edged and veined black. ♀ has black apical patch with two rows of spots which may be red, white or violet and white. *Colotis ione* ♂ has small apical black patch enclosing five or six purple spots: *Colotis erone* ♂ is smaller with only three purple spots in apical patch.
Range and Habitat A savannah and bush country white which ranges locally from Central and Eastern Africa south to Natal and Transvaal, South Africa. Flies throughout the year.

COLOTIS HETAERA Gerstaecker   p 80
Crimson Tip

Identification Wingspan 5½–6½cm. ♂ white with a dark grey apical patch enclosing five elongated crimson spots. ♀ white or pale yellow; apical half of forewings black with three pale spots and a broad black marginal band on hindwing. *Colotis eunoma* has two or three crimson spots in apical patch.
Range and Habitat Inhabits wooded areas and coastal bush in Kenya and Tanzania: not uncommon in Sokoke–Arabuku Forest on Kenya coast. Flies throughout the year.

COLOTIS EUNOMA Hopffer   p 80
Three Spot Crimson Tip
Identification Wingspan 5–6½cm. ♂ white or creamy white with three, sometimes four,

elongated crimson spots in apex of forewing; these may or may not be enclosed in a grey apical patch. ♀ yellowish-cream with dark grey markings and row of post-discal spots in forewing: two or three crimson spots in apical patch. *Colotis hetaera* ♂ has five crimson apical spots and ♀ lacks row of forewing spots.

Range and Habitat A very local and uncommon species recorded from Kenya, south through eastern Tanzania to Mozambique. Inhabits littoral sand dunes, lightly wooded areas and coastal bush. Flies throughout the year.

COLOTIS ELGONENSIS E. Sharpe
Elgon Crimson Tip

p 80

Identification Wingspan 4–4½cm. ♂ white with narrow grey apical patch containing two or three small pale crimson spots. ♀ resembles ♂ but lacks crimson spots. Species distinguished from related species by small size and restricted apical patch.

4cm

Range and Habitat A forest species found in the highlands of Kenya, Uganda and Tanzania, and the Bamenda Highlands, Cameroons. Flies throughout the year.

COLOTIS HILDEBRANDTI Staudinger
Golden Tip

p 80

Identification Wingspan 4½–6cm. ♂ white with apical half of forewing orange-gold edged black; hindwing with broken marginal black band; base of wings grey. ♀ yellow washed orange, with brown apical patch enclosing orange-gold spots; base of wings brown and band of brown spots on hindwing.

Range and Habitat Woodland and savannah and coastal bush in Kenya, Tanzania and Malawi. A local species but common in acacia woodland at Voi, eastern Kenya. Flies throughout the year.

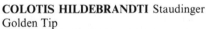

COLOTIS DANAE Fabricius   p 80
Scarlet Tip

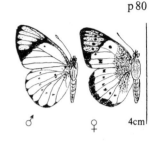

Identification Wingspan 4–5cm. ♂ white
with very large carmine-red apical forewing patch bordered by black margin:
triangular marginal black spots on hindwing. ♀ has red apical patch divided by
row of black spots; brownish grey basal
suffusion: post-discal row of spots on
hindwing. Underside of hindwing with
post-discal row of spots present in ♂
and ♀. Dry season insects are less heavily marked.

Range and Habitat Common throughout most of the Ethiopian Region,
inhabiting woodlands, edge of forests, savannah and bush country and open
grasslands. Flies throughout the year.

Larval Food Plants Various species of *Cadaba*.

COLOTIS EUCHARIS Fabricius   p 81
Sulphur Orange Tip

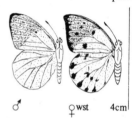

Identification Wingspan 3–4½cm. ♂ wet
season form, yellow with large orange
apical patch on forewing: ♀ with brown
markings, a black spot in forewing cell
and marginal brown spots on hindwing.
In the dry season forms the ground colour
is creamy white, not yellow, and in the ♀
dark markings are less extensive.

Range and Habitat Widely distributed through Ethiopian Region, outside
forest areas. Inhabits bush country and semi-desert areas. Flight relatively
weak, much attracted to flowering plants and bushes. On wing throughout
the year.

Larval Food Plants Various species of *Capparis*.

COLOTIS ANTEVIPPE Boisduval   p 81
Red Tip

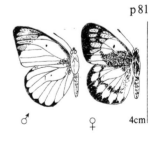

Identification Wingspan 3½–5cm. ♂ white,
with a bright red apical patch with a
straight inner edge; black margin to
hindwing: black bar along lower edge of
forewing in wet season forms: small black
spot in cell of forewing. ♀ white or yellowish with orange or red apical spots, and

wings with heavy brown or blackish markings. Veins of underside darkened. Species exhibits much seasonal variation. In *Colotis evenina* the apical patch is orange, and in ♀ the black forewing bar slants upwards. *Colotis euippe* has forewings rounded and inner edge of red apical patch curved.

Range and Habitat Common in bush, savannah and grasslands throughout Ethiopian Region. Flies throughout the year.

Larval Food Plants Various species of Capparidaceae.

COLOTIS EVENINA Wallengren   p 81

African Orange Tip

Identification Wingspan 4–5½cm. ♂ white with an orange apical patch: dark markings variable, sparse in dry season, heavy in wet season forms. ♀ white or yellowish, distinguished from related forms by upwards slanting black forewing bar: dark markings variable according to season.

Range and Habitat Inhabits open and bush country; common but local over greater part of Ethiopian Region. Flies throughout the year.

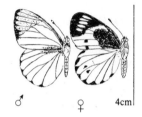

♂   ♀   4cm

COLOTIS EUIPPE Linnaeus   p 81

Smoky Orange Tip

Identification Wingspan 3–4½cm. Forewings rounded: ♂ white, red apical patch edged black; blackish-brown bar on hindwing; ♀ white or yellowish with variable dark markings: no black spot in forewing cell in either ♂ or ♀.

Range and Habitat Common species throughout Ethiopian Region in open bush country and grasslands. Flies throughout the year.

Larval Food Plants Various species of Capparidaceae.

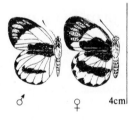

♂   ♀   4cm

COLOTIS PALLENE Hopffer p81
Bushvelt Orange Tip

Identification Wingspan 2½–4cm. Seasonally variable. ♂ white with orange-red
apical patch; black dot in forewing cell.
♀ very similar to *Colotis euippe* but with
black spot in forewing cell. *Colotis pallene*
may be distinguished by having a yellow,
not red, apical patch on underside of forewing.

4cm

Range and Habitat Dry bush country in South Africa, South-West Africa
and Rhodesia and Malawi.

COLOTIS AGOYE Wallengren p81
Speckled Sulphur Tip

Identification Wingspan 3½–4½cm. Apex of forewings very acute. ♂ white, with or without blackened veins, finely speckled with black scales in
extreme wet season form; apical patch ochreous-
orange; underside white. ♀ similar to ♂ but
in wet season form veins blackened only on
terminal half of wings and apical patch duller
and larger.

♂ 4cm

Range and Habitat Inhabits arid bush country
in South Africa, South-West Africa and Som-
alia: local and uncommon. In South Africa perhaps most plentiful at Saltpan,
Zoutpansberg, northern Transvaal. Flies throughout the year.

COLOTIS EVAGORE Klug p81
Small Orange Tip

Identification Wingspan 3–4cm. Seasonally very
variable. ♂ white, with orange-red apical patch
with a black notch on its inner edge; ♀ white or
yellowish, apical spots variable, .red, yellowish
or whitish. Orange-red apical patch on underside of forewing in both sexes.

Range and Habitat A common species throughout Ethiopian Region in open country, bush and
grasslands. Flies throughout the year.

♂ ♀ 4cm

Larval Food Plants Various species of Capparidaceae, including *Cadaba*, *Capparis* and *Maerua*.

COLOTIS ERIS Klug   p 81
Banded Gold Tip

Identification Wingspan 4–5½cm. ♂
white with a pale lilac-brown apical
patch enclosing four or five golden-
buff spots; black bar across inner
margin of forewing and across upper
part of hindwing. ♀ white or dull
yellowish with pale spotted apical
patch: in wet season form blackish-
brown band across inner margin of
forewing.

Range and Habitat Widely distributed
throughout Ethiopian Region except
more arid regions of South-West Africa and Cape Province, South Africa.
Inhabits open bush country and savannah. Very rapid flier, not easily netted
unless visiting flowering shrubs. Flies throughout the year.

Larval Food Plants Various species of *Capparis*.

COLOTIS SUBFASCIATUS Swainson   p 81
Lemon Traveller

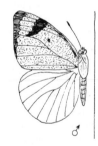

Identification Wingspan 5–6cm. ♂ forewings sulphur-yellow with blackish-brown border; hindwings whitish; black band present on forewing,
forming an incomplete apical patch; black spot in
forewing cell. ♀ variable, with pale yellow or yellowish-white forewings; orange-red apical patch. Dry
season specimens have reduced and paler dark
markings.

Range and Habitat Inhabits dry bush country from
northern Tanzania southwards to Malawi, Zambia,
Rhodesia to northern Transvaal and Orange
Free State, South Africa, westwards to Angola.
An extremely swift and strong flier, difficult to
capture unless visiting flowers. Flies throughout the
year.

ERONIA CLEODORA Hubner   p 65
Vine Leaf Vagrant

Identification Wingspan 5–7cm. White, or creamy-white, with a broad but
variable blackish-brown marginal band

on fore and hindwings; two white apical spots; underside hindwing with dead leaf pattern. Sexes similar but ♀ usually more yellowish-white.

Range and Habitat Widely distributed from Angola and Congo in west, Ethiopia, Uganda and Kenya in east, southwards to South Africa. Inhabits open woodlands, savannah and bush country. Flies throughout the year.

Larval Food Plants *Capparis*.

ERONIA LEDA Boisduval
Orange and Lemon

p 65

Identification Wingspan 5–6cm. ♂ bright yellow with apical half of forewings orange; resembles a larger edition of *Colotis eucharis* but brighter. ♀ variable, whitish to pale yellow, with or without orange apical patch; some brown marking on apex of forewing.

Range and Habitat A local species found in East Africa to South Africa and Angola; inhabits bush country, savannah and open woodlands: a swift flier, difficult to net unless visiting flowers. On the wing throughout the year.

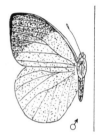

NEPHERONIA THALASSINA Boisduval
Cambridge Vagrant

p 65

Identification Wingspan 5½–6cm. ♂ white, strongly tinged greenish-blue; black apex and margin to forewings: hindwings with or without black marginal spots. ♀ variable, may be creamy-white, yellowish-white with white hindwings or white with yellowish hindwings; black apical patch and margin to forewings, hindwings with marginal spots. Underside with pearly gloss.

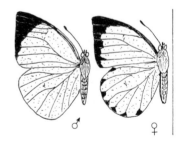

Range and Habitat West, Central and East Africa south to Transvaal in South Africa. Inhabits wooded areas and forests. Flight strong and fast, often flying high and not easy to net. The pale greenish-blue males are very conspicuous. Flies throughout the year.

p 65

NEPHERONIA ARGIA Fabricius
Large Vagrant

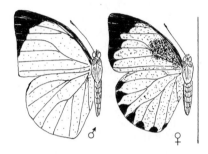

Identification Wingspan 7–8 cm. ♂ white to pale bluish-white with black apical patch: underside without silky sheen. ♀ very variable, white, yellow or orange-yellow; with or without orange basal patch in fore-wing; black apical patch and marginal markings.

Range and Habitat Widely distributed over much of the Ethiopian Region, south to Natal and eastern Cape Province, South Africa and north-ern South-West Africa. Inhabits forests, wooded areas and dense coastal bush. Strong flier, not easy to net. On wing throughout the year.

COLIAS ELECTO Linnaeus   p 65
African Clouded Yellow

Identification Wingspan 4–5cm. ♂ rich orange with a broad dark brown marginal border; orange-red spot in cell of hindwing. ♀ occurs in two forms; one like the ♂ but with yellow spots in the dark border, the other in which the ground colour is pale greenish-white.

Range and Habitat Common over much of Africa, frequenting grasslands, lucerne fields, edges of forest, open woodland and mountain moorlands. Flight strong and direct. Flies throughout the year.

Larval Food Plants Mainly various Leguminosae (Papilionaceae), *Vicia*, *Cytisus*. Sometimes a pest on lucerne.

♂   4cm

ACRAEIDAE & DANAIDAE – ACRAEAS & MONARCHS

1   **ACRAEA PERENNA** ♂   *page* 118
    Sexes similar: with or without black forewing suffusion.
2   **ACRAEA ACRITA** ♂   115
    Sexes similar: black spotting variable.
3   **ACRAEA SEMIVITREA** ♂   120
    Sexes similar: wings largely transparent.
4   **ACRAEA NATALICA** ♂   116
    ♀ browner or greyer than ♂: hindwing marginal band sometimes very
    broad.
5   **ACRAEA ASBOLOPLINTHA** ♂   116
    ♀ has browner hindwing: eastern race has red or (♀) whitish forewing
    band spotted with black.
6   **ACRAEA SATIS** ♂ ♀   109
    Irregular black band across hindwing.
7   **ACRAEA ANEMOSA** ♂ ♀   114
    Hindwing, black marginal band unspotted.
8   **ACRAEA PSEUDOLYCIA** ♂   114
    Sexes similar: black spots on hindwing.
9   **BEMATISTES AGANICE** ♂ ♀   107
    Variable: forewing band not reaching inner margin.
10 **BEMATISTES ALCINOE** ♂ ♀   106
    ♀, hindwing basal patch reddish.
11 **AMAURIS ALBIMACULATA** ♂   104
    Underside abdomen whitish.
12 **DANAUS CHRYSIPPUS** ♂ ♂ ♂   100
    Sexes similar: ♀ with three black dots on hindwing.
13 **DANAUS LIMNIACE** ♂   101
    Sexes similar.
14 **DANAUS FORMOSA FORMOSA** ♂   101
    Sexes similar: basal area forewing orange-brown.
15 **DANAUS FORMOSA MERCEDOINA** ♂   101
    Sexes similar: basal areas forewing dark red-brown.
16 **AMAURIS NIAVIUS** ♂   102
    Sexes similar: margin of hindwing unspotted.
17 **AMAURIS OCHLEA** ♂   103
    Sexes similar: large white hindwing patch.

PLATE 10   97

NYMPHALIDAE – EUXANTHE, CHARAXES

1 **EUXANTHE TRAJANUS** ♂   *page* 123
Sexes similar, but ♀ with yellowish hindwing patch.

2 **EUXANTHE TIBERIUS** ♂ ♀   124
♂ hindwing black without pale patch.

3 **EUXANTHE CROSSLEYI** ♂   125
Sexes similar: hindwing with extensive pale markings.

4 **EUXANTHE EURINOME** ♂ ♀   125
Hindwing with restricted pale markings.

5 **EUXANTHE WAKEFIELDI** ♂ ♀   124
♂ with vivid blue-green markings: ♀ black and white.

6 **CHARAXES CANDIOPE** ♂   127
♀ larger with longer tails.

7 **CHARAXES ACUMINATUS** ♂   126
Sexes similar: tip of forewing attenuated.

8 **CHARAXES FULVESCENS** ♂   126
Sexes similar: tip of forewing not attenuated.

9 **CHARAXES VARANES** ♂   125
Sexes similar: basal areas pearly-white.

CATOPSILIA FLORELLA Fabricius   p 81
African Migrant

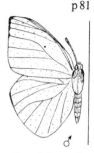

Identification Wingspan 5½–7cm. ♂ very pale greenish-white with a small elongate dot at the end of
the forewing cell; little or no brown at apex of forewing. ♀ sulphur-yellow with round dark spot in
forewing cell; apex and upper margin of forewing
with small rufous-brown markings; underside
deeper yellow with three small brown rings in centre
of hindwings and indistinct, fine brown vermicula-
tions.

Range and Habitat One of the commonest butterflies in Africa, found throughout in a variety of habitats from open grasslands and bush to margins of forest.
Flight direct and strong: often migratory. Flies throughout the year.

Larval Food Plants Various species of *Cassia* (Leguminosae), including cultivated species.

EUREMA HECABE Linnaeus   p 65
Common Grass Yellow

Identification Wingspan 3–4cm. Seasonally variable; bright yellow with a blackish apex and
border to forewing angled inwards below apex;
hindwing with marginal spots, sometimes a
narrow marginal band. Sexes similar but ♀
usually larger.

Range and Habitat A weak flying species
common throughout Ethiopian Region, in-
habitating open grasslands, cultivation and

♂   4cm

garden, and bush and savannah country. Flies throughout the year.

Larval Food Plants *Hypericum, Cassia, Aeschynomene, Lespedeza* and other
Leguminosae.

EUREMA BRIGITTA Cramer   p 65
Broad-bordered Grass Yellow

Identification Wingspan 2½–3½cm. Variable;
yellow or dusky yellow with a broad black or
brown border to both wings; forewing band
curved but not sharply angled inwards as in
Eurema hecabe. Sexes similar, but ♀ usually
larger than ♂.

Range and Habitat Widespread and common

♂   4cm

throughout Ethiopian Region in open country, bush, cultivation and gardens. Flight weak, often settles. Often gathers in masses at roadside puddles. Flies throughout the year.
Larval Food Plants *Hypericum*.

EUREMA HAPALE Mabille   p 65
Pale Grass Yellow
Identification Wingspan 2½–3½cm. Very pale yellow or yellowish-white with a very restricted brown or blackish apical patch. Sexes alike, but ♀ usually larger and some examples have slightly larger apical patch.
Range and Habitat Widely distributed in West, Central and East Africa, south to Mozambique and north-eastern Rhodesia. Less common than previous two species; inhabits damper areas, especially marshy grasslands and margins of streams. Flies throughout the year.

♂   4cm

EUREMA DESJARDINSI Boisduval   p 65
Angled Grass Yellow
Identification Wingspan 2½–4cm. Yellow with a black or dark brown apex and border: hindwing with a very narrow black border or with marginal dots: hindwing distinctly angled. Sexes similar, but ♀ often larger with slightly wider apical markings.
Range and Habitat A common and widespread species in all types of open country throughout Ethiopian Region. A weak flier, often congregates around muddy puddles. On wing throughout the year.
Larval Food Plants Reputed to lay on *Hypericum*.

♂   4cm

FAMILY DANAIDAE
MONARCHS

The butterflies of this Family, represented by some 14 species in Africa, are medium or large-sized insects. They are remarkable for their extreme tenacity of life, being difficult to kill by pinching the thorax.

The Monarchs, or Milkweed Butterflies as they are sometimes called, are reputedly distasteful to bird and lizard predators, exuding an acrid fluid when captured. Certain butterflies of other groups which are palatable to vertebrate predators, for example the Papilios, mimic the colour pattern and slow, sailing flight of their Danaid 'models'.

Characters distinguishing this group include wings large for the size of the body; head and thorax marked with white dots; first pair of legs greatly reduced; presence of a patch of scent scales on hindwing of ♂; cells of both fore and hindwings closed.

Early Stages. The longitudinally ribbed eggs are laid on leaves or young shoots of plants of the milkweed family, Asclepiadaceae. The larvae are smooth, often with brightly coloured bands, and are ornamented with long fleshy filaments growing from their backs. In several species the larvae are gregarious. The pupae are smooth and barrel-shaped, often with metallic patches: they hang free, suspended by the tail.

The butterflies appear on the wing throughout the year, except in the colder parts of their range in southern Africa where they fly generally from October to May.

DANAUS CHRYSIPPUS Linnaeus p 96
African Monarch
Identification Wingspan 7–8½ cm. A black-margined orange-brown butterfly with a large triangular black apical patch enclosing white spots: hindwing with or without a large white patch: a second form lacks the black apical patch; it also may or may not possess a white hindwing patch. The ♀ of

Hypolimnas misippus mimics this species. (See plate 21).

Range and Habitat A very common species throughout the Ethiopian Region. Inhabits open and bush country, gardens and woodlands and margins of forests. Flight slow and sailing. Flies throughout the year.
Larval Food Plants Various species of Asclepiadaceae, the milkweed family.

DANAUS LIMNIACE Cramer   p96
Blue Monarch

Identification Wingspan 7–9cm. A large black butterfly with numerous semi-translucent blue spots and streaks. Sexes similar. This species is mimicked by the swallowtail *Graphium leonidas*. (Plate 5.)
Range and Habitat A common and widely distributed species in West, Central and East Africa as far south as Rhodesia. Occurs in wooded areas, forests and gardens. Has a slow, gliding flight about six to ten feet above the ground.
Larval Food Plants Various Asclepiadaceae.

DANAUS FORMOSA Godman   p96
Beautiful Monarch

Identification Wingspan 7–9cm. A large white-spotted black butterfly with basal third of forewing pale orange-brown or deep rufous; submarginal bands of white or cream spots on hindwing, and a creamy-white basal area. This species is mimicked by the swallowtail *Papilio rex*.
Range and Habitat Distributed from West Africa and the Congo, east to Ethiopia, Uganda, Kenya and Tanzania. Inhabits wooded areas, forests and gardens. A high sailing flight. Flies throughout the year.
Larval Food Plants Various Asclepiadaceae.

AMAURIS ANSORGEI E. Sharpe
Ansorge's Danaid

Identification Wingspan 8cm. A black and white species with an extensive golden-yellow patch on hindwing. Sexes similar. In race found in the eastern Congo and western Uganda all pale markings bright golden yellow. This insect has been treated as a distinct species, *Amauris ellioti*.

Range and Habitat A high forest species of Kenya Highlands, to eastern Congo, south to Malawi. Characteristic buoyant, sailing flight: locally common and often gregarious. Flies throughout the year.

AMAURIS NIAVIUS Linnaeus
Friar

p 96

Identification Wingspan $8\frac{1}{2}$–10cm. A large black or blackish-brown butterfly with large white patches on fore and hindwings: no white submarginal spots in hindwing. *Amauris ochlea* differs in having a wide white band on forewing and white submarginal spots on hindwing. Sexes similar. Species mimicked by certain ♀ forms of *Papilio dardanus* and *Hypolimnas dubius*.

Range and Habitat Widely distributed in Ethiopian Region, south to Natal and Transvaal, South Africa. Inhabits forests and wooded country. On the wing throughout the year.

AMAURIS TARTAREA Mabille
Monk

Identification Wingspan 7–$8\frac{1}{2}$cm. A large black and white butterfly with a broken white band on forewing and a large white hindwing patch. Sexes alike.

Amauris ochlea has a complete forewing band; *Amauris hecate* has a much smaller hindwing patch.

Range and Habitat A common and widely distributed forest species in West, Central and East Africa, but not in Ethiopia or South Africa. Flies throughout the year.

AMAURIS OCHLEA Boisduval
Novice

p 96

Identification Wingspan 7–8½ cm. A large black and white species usually with an unbroken white forewing band and large white hindwing patch. Sexes alike. *Amauris tartarea* has forewing band broken into three spots.

Range and Habitat Occurs in lowland woodland and forest in eastern Africa from Somalia south to Natal, South Africa. Species often flies in shady places: on the wing throughout the year.

Larval Food Plants *Tylophora*, *Cyanchum*.

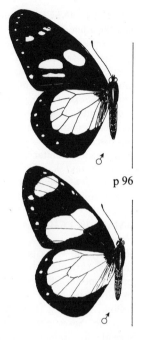

AMAURIS HECATE Butler
Dusky Danaid

Identification Wingspan 6½–8 cm. Forewing black with white bar and spots; hindwing black with much reduced white basal patch. *Amauris tartarea* has a much larger white hindwing patch. Sexes alike.

Range and Habitat A West African forest species which extends eastwards to Uganda, western Kenya and Ethiopia. Flies throughout the year.

AMAURIS INFERNA Butler
Identification Wingspan 6–7½
cm. Forewing black with white
spots: hindwing black with
restricted ochreous discal area
gradually merging into dark
border. Sexes alike. *Amauris
echeria* and *Amauris albimaculata* have clearly defined ochreous discal patches.
Range and Habitat A forest
species found locally in West
Africa, the Congo and Uganda.
Flies throughout the year.

AMAURIS ECHERIA Stoll
Chief
Identification Wingspan 6–7½cm. An extremely variable velvety black or dark
brown species; the spots on the forewing
usually white, but in some races ochreous-
yellow; hindwing patch may be narrow
or wide. Sexes alike. Some races very
similar to *Amauris albimaculata* but
underside of abdomen dark in *A. echeria*,
whitish in *A. albimaculata*; the underside
of the palps with a white spot in *A. echeria*,
a white stripe present in *A. albimaculata*.
Both species are mimicked by ♀♀ of
swallowtails *Papilio echerioides* and
Papilio jacksoni.

Range and Habitat Widely distributed in forested regions, heavy woodland
and bush in West Africa, the Congo, eastwards to Uganda, Ethiopia and
Kenya, south to South Africa. Flies throughout the year.
Larval Food Plants *Cynanchum*, *Tylophora*.

AMAURIS ALBIMACULATA Butler   p 96
Layman
Identification Wingspan 6½–7½cm. Black or dark brown, always with forewings white spotted; rectangular ochreous-yellow patch on hindwing, pale
in some races. Sexes alike. Some races very similar to *Amauris echeria*, but

distinguished by whitish underside of abdomen, and white stripe, not a dot, on underside of palps.

Range and Habitat Eastern Congo to southern Sudan, Uganda and Kenya, south to Natal, South Africa: isolated population in Cameroons, West Africa. Inhabits forests and heavy woodlands. Flies throughout the year.

Larval Food Plants *Tylophora, Cynanchum.*

FAMILY ACRAEIDAE
ACRAEAS

The Acraeas are a family of medium-sized butterflies related to the Monarchs, with long narrow wings and slow, buoyant flight. Like the Monarchs they are distasteful to predators. Their predominant colours are red and orange.

Structural characters include the absence of an abdominal flap to the hindwing, and a closed cell in both fore and hindwings; there are no scent scale patches on the wings; abdomen usually elongated.

Certain species of the genus *Pseudacraea* (Nymphalidae) are so strongly mimetic of some species of Acraeas of the genus *Bematistes* that there is difficulty in distinguishing between them except on the structural character of an open hindwing cell in *Pseudacraea*.

Early Stages. The eggs are laid singly or in clusters, in many cases on leaves of some species of Passifloraceae including cultivated passion flowers and grenadillas. The larvae are cylindrical with longitudinal rows of rigid branched spines, as in some of the Nymphalids, but the arrangement is different and there are no spines on the head. They are often gregarious, especially in the first or second instars. The pupae are long and slender, with dark markings but without metallic patches; with or without abdominal spines. The perfect insects are on the wing throughout the year, except in colder parts of their range, but are most abundant during and after rains.

BEMATISTES ALCINOE Felder   p 96

Identification Wingspan 7–9½cm. ♂ blackish-brown with orange-brown forewing and hindwing bands: ♀ larger than ♂, blackish-brown and white

with small black spots in basal area of hindwing. The similar *Bematistes aganice* has a shorter forewing band.

Range and Habitat West Africa from Sierra Leone to the Cameroons, eastwards through the Congo to Uganda and western Kenya. A forest species: often flies high and attracted to flowering trees such as Albizia. On the wing throughout the year.

BEMATISTES UMBRA Drury

Identification Wingspan 7–9½cm. ♂ black or blackish-brown with serrated orange-red forewing band; white band on hindwing. ♀ larger than ♂, blackish-brown with jagged white band on forewing and white band on hindwing.

Range and Habitat A West African forest species which extends eastwards through the Congo to Uganda and western Kenya. On the wing throughout the year.

BEMATISTES AGANICE Hewitson   p 96
Wanderer

Identification Wingspan 6–8cm. ♂ blackish-brown with pale yellow to orange-brown markings. ♀ with pale ochreous yellow to white bands; hindwing basal patch reddish.

Range and Habitat A forest and heavy woodland species from Ethiopia southwards through Uganda and Kenya to Mozambique, Malawi, Zambia and Rhodesia to South Africa. Flies throughout the year.
Larval Food Plants *Passiflora*, *Adenia* and *Ophiocaulon*.

BEMATISTES SCALIVITTATA Butler

Identification Wingspan 7–8½ cm. Blackish-brown to black with very reduced white markings on forewing: small, ill-defined pale ochreous patch on hindwing. Sexes alike.
Range and Habitat An uncommon species found in mountain forests of Malawi and southern Tanzania. Flies throughout the year.

BEMATISTES QUADRICOLOR Rogenhofer

Identification Wingspan 7cm. Forewing with a rich red-brown basal area, an orange median band and a black apex: hindwing black with a white or pale buff band. Sexes similar but ♀ usually larger.
Range and Habitat Mountain forests of Kenya, western Uganda, south to central Tanzania. An uncommon and local insect. Flies throughout the year.

BEMATISTES POGGEI Dewitz

Identification Wingspan 7½–8 cm. Black with a broad orange band on forewing: white band on hindwing. Sexes alike.
Range and Habitat A West African forest species which occurs from Angola through the Congo to Uganda, western Kenya and Ethiopia. Flies throughout the year.

BEMATISTES MACARISTA
Identification Wingspan 7½–9cm. Forewing acute; ♂ black with bright red-brown forewing band; whitish band on hindwing: ♀ blackish-brown with white bands on both fore and hindwings. Some ♂♂ have a trace of orange on hindwing band.

Range and Habitat A common forest species from West Africa through the Congo to Uganda and western Kenya.

♂   ♀

ACRAEA SATIS Ward   p 96
Coast Acraea

Identification Wingspan 7–8cm. ♂ bright red with black markings; apex and margin of forewing translucent with veins blackened. ♀ like ♂ but red areas replaced by white: irregular black band across hindwing in both sexes.

Range and Habitat Not uncommon in forest and woodland in coastal areas from Kenya south to Natal, South Africa: also occurs in eastern Rhodesia. A very

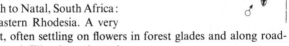

slow-flying insect, often settling on flowers in forest glades and along roadways: easily captured. Flies throughout the year.

ACRAEA PENTAPOLIS Ward
Identification Wingspan 7–7½cm. Wings mainly transparent with lightly scaled brown markings on forewing: yellowish-orange around cell of hindwing and at inner margin. Sexes alike but ♀ usually larger. The closely related *Acraea vesperalis* has the hindwing brownish-orange without transparent area.

♂

Range and Habitat Forests of West Africa from Sierra Leone, through the Congo to Uganda: also inland areas of Tanzania to Mozambique and Malawi. Flies throughout the year.

ACRAEA VESPERALIS Grose-Smith

Identification Wingspan 6–6½cm. Forewings transparent with lightly scaled brownish markings: hindwings orange-brown with dark brown border: no transparent area. Sexes similar. *Acraea pentapolis* has a transparent area on hindwing.

Range and Habitat A forest species ranging from West Africa and the Congo to Uganda. Flies throughout the year.

ACRAEA ITURINA Grose-Smith

Identification Wingspan 6cm. Forewings bright red with large transparent area; black spot in cell; hindwings bright red with heavy black markings and a dusky border. Sexes alike.

Range and Habitat West African forests from the Cameroons, through the Congo to Uganda; an isolated race in Ethiopia. Flies throughout the year.

ACRAEA QUIRINA Fabricius

Identification Wingspan 6–6½cm. ♂ forewing almost completely transparent with red patch at base; hindwing bright red with black spots and a transparent marginal border. ♀ similar to ♂ but larger and hindwing reddish-brown not bright red.

Range and Habitat A common forest and woodland species in West Africa and the Congo, east to Uganda, Kenya and Tanzania. Flies throughout the year.

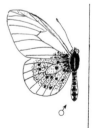

ACRAEA ADMATHA Hewitson
Identification Wingspan 5½–6cm. ♂ forewing bright red with large apical patch
transparent; hindwing red with black
spots and black marginal border spotted
with red : ♀ slightly larger and red replaced
by reddish-brown or grey.
Range and Habitat A common and widely
distributed species from West Africa and
the Congo to Ethiopia, south through

Uganda, Kenya and Tanzania to South Africa. Inhabits forests, heavy woodland and coastal bush. Flies throughout the year.

ACRAEA TERPSICORE Linnaeus
Neobule Acraea
Identification Wingspan 5–6cm. ♂ forewing pale orange-red with black spots;
transparent patch below apex; hindwing
red, spotted with black; red-spotted
black marginal border. ♀ slightly larger
and orange-brown, not red.
Range and Habitat A common species
throughout the Ethiopian Region, inhabiting dry bush country, savannah and
wooded areas. Flies throughout the year.
Larval Food Plants *Adenia, Passiflora.*

ACRAEA ZETES Linnaeus
Large Spotted Acraea
Identification Wingspan 6–7½cm. Wings
red with heavy black markings, a black
apical patch and a black marginal band
on hindwing. Specimens from West
Africa, the Congo and Uganda have
blackish suffusion over forewings; those
from eastern and South Africa brighter

red with little or no black suffusion. Sexes similar but ♀ usually larger.
Range and Habitat A common species found over most of the Ethiopian
Region. Inhabits bush and savannah country, woodlands, forest margins and
coastal scrub.
Larval Food Plants *Adenia, Passiflora.*

NYMPHALIDAE – CHARAXES

1 **CHARAXES PROTOCLEA PROTOCLEA** ♂ ♀   *page* 127
   Restricted red markings.

2 **CHARAXES BOUETI** ♂ ♀   130
   No silvery-white band on underside hindwing.

3 **CHARAXES PROTOCLEA AZOTA** ♂ ♀   130
   Extensive red markings.

4 **CHARAXES LASTI** ♂ ♀   130
   Narrow silvery-white transverse band on underside hindwing.

5 **CHARAXES LACTITINCTUS** ♂ ♀   131
   Silvery-blue basal areas.

6 **CHARAXES BRUTUS** ♂   134
   Sexes similar but ♀ larger with longer tails.

7 **CHARAXES POLLUX** ♂   134
   Sexes similar but ♀ larger with longer tails.

8 **CHARAXES CYNTHIA** ♂ ♀   131
   ♂ without purplish bloom: narrow silvery-white transverse band on
   underside hindwing.

9 **CHARAXES LUCRETIUS** ♂ ♀   131
   ♂ with distinct purplish bloom: no silvery-white band on underside
   hindwing.

1

2

3 ♂

3 ♀

4

5

6 ♂

6 ♀

7 ♂

7 ♀

8 ♂

8 ♀

9

10 ♂

10 ♀

11

PLATE 12 · 113

NYMPHALIDAE – CHARAXES

1 **CHARAXES JASIUS EPIJASIUS** ♂ *page* 132
Sexes similar but ♀ larger with longer tails: no pale bands on forewing:
blue patch on hindwing.

2 **CHARAXES JASIUS SATURNUS** ♂ 132
Sexes similar but ♀ larger with longer tails: pale bands on forewing:
blue spots on hindwing.

3 **CHARAXES ANSORGEI** ♂ ♀ 134
White hindwing band.

4 **CHARAXES PHOEBUS** ♂ 135
Sexes similar but ♀ larger with slightly longer tails: wide pale margin
fore and hindwings

5 **CHARAXES NICHETES** ♂ 159
Sexes similar: forewing deeply concave: no tails.

6 **CHARAXES CASTOR** ♂ ♀ 133
Dark brown with orange-buff or creamy-buff transverse bands.

7 **CHARAXES DRUCEANUS** ♂ ♀ 135
Underside with extensive silvery-white markings.

8 **CHARAXES BAUMANNI** ♂ ♀ 150

9 **CHARAXES PELIAS** ♂ 132
Sexes similar: shorter, thicker tails than *Charaxes jasius saturnus*, and
underside mainly grey not red-brown.

10 **CHARAXES EUDOXUS** ♂ ♀ 136
Forewing extensively black.

11 **CHARAXES HANSALI** ♂ 133
Sexes similar but ♀ larger with longer tails: dark greyish-brown to
blackish with creamy-white bands.

ACRAEA ANEMOSA Hewitson   p 96
Broad-bordered Acraea

Identification Wingspan 6–7cm. Forewing rich orange-brown to dark rich red,
with black apical patch and markings;
hindwing with blackish base and very
broad unspotted black margin; no black
spots. Sexes similar but ♀ larger and
slightly duller. The similar *Acraea pseudolycia* has black spots on hindwing.
Range and Habitat A wide-ranging species
in Ethiopian Region, inhabiting thorn bush and savannah country, wooded
areas and coastal scrub. Flies throughout the year.
Larval Food Plants *Modecca.*

ACRAEA PSEUDOLYCIA Butler   p 96
Identification Wingspan 6–7cm. Forewing reddish-brown, paler in ♀, with
black markings and apical patch; hindwing reddish-brown with black spots;
broad black margin with or without spots.
The similar *Acraea anemosa* has no black
spots on hindwing.

Range and Habitat Ranges from Angola
eastwards to Rhodesia, north to southern
Sudan, Uganda, Ethiopia, Kenya and
Tanzania. Inhabits bush and savannah country and light woodland. On the
wing throughout the year.

ACRAEA EGINA Mabille
Elegant Acraea
Identification Wingspan 7–8cm. ♂♀ bright
red with heavy black markings and apical
half of forewings dusted with black
scales: the eastern and southern race is
orange-brown and lacks this black suffusion; hindwing red with black spots;
unspotted black margin.
Range and Habitat Forests and well-
wooded localities throughout Ethiopian
Region south to Mozambique and Rhodesia.

ACRAEA ACRITA Hewitson   p 96
Fiery Acraea

Identification Wingspan 5½–6½cm. ♂
bright vermilion red with a small black
apical tip, a few scattered black spots and
a red-spotted black hindwing margin. ♀
variable, from orange-red to greyish-
brown. A variable species as to extent and
size of black markings.
Range and Habitat An open country,
bush and savannah species found in
Kenya and Tanzania, south to Mozambique and Rhodesia, west to the
southern Congo and Angola. Flies throughout the year.

ACRAEA CALDARENA Hewitson
Black-tipped Acraea

Identification Wingspan 4½–5½cm. ♂ pale
pink, rather sparsely scaled, with a broad
black apical patch; small rounded black
dots on fore and hindwings; narrow black
hindwing margin with pink spots. ♀ duller
and browner. Race found along Kenya–
Tanzania coast has a smaller black apical
patch.
Range and Habitat An open country and bush acraea found in Kenya,
Uganda and Tanzania, south to Natal, South Africa.
Larval Food Plants *Wormskjoldia.*

ACRAEA ONCAEA Hopffer
Window Acraea

Identification Wingspan 4½–5cm. ♂ light
red, rather thinly scaled on forewing,
with dark streaks below apex; narrow
black apical patch and black spots on both
wings: narrow dark hindwing border
with reddish spots. ♀ pale or dark brown,
often with a white subapical band on forewing.
Range and Habitat Dry bush country
from Ethiopia south through Kenya and
Tanzania to Transvaal and Natal, South Africa. Flies throughout the year.
Larval Food Plants *Adenia, Oncoba, Wormskjoldia* and *Xylotheca.*

ACRAEA NATALICA Boisduval
Natal Acraea

p 96

Identification Wingspan 5–6½cm. ♂ red with heavy black basal markings; black apical patch and black hindwing margin; ♀ like ♂ but brownish red, or sometimes dark grey.

Range and Habitat A common species of bush and savannah country, and woodland throughout Ethiopian Region. Flies throughout the year.

Larval Food Plants *Passiflora*, *Adenia* and *Wormskjoldia*.

ACRAEA ASBOLOPLINTHA Karsch
Black-winged Acraea

p 96

Identification Wingspan 5½–6cm. ♂ forewing black, rather lightly scaled; hindwing bright red with small black basal patch and a few black spots: ♀ like ♂ but with red-brown hindwing. The race found in highlands of eastern Kenya has a black-spotted red band on forewing in ♂; and a dusky white band in the ♀.

Range and Habitat Forests, wooded areas and gardens from eastern Congo to Uganda and Kenya. Flies throughout the year.

Larval Food Plants *Passiflora*.

ACRAEA ENCEDON Linnaeus
White-barred Acraea

Identification Wingspan 5–5½cm. Variaable, a mimic of *Danaus chrysippus*: pale ochreous-yellow to light brown with a broad black apex crossed by a white apical bar; narrow black marginal border to hindwing: some examples lack the black and white apical patch: in others the ground colour is dusky white.

Range and Habitat A common species

throughout the Ethiopian Region in a variety of habitats, from bush to forest.
Flies throughout the year.
Larval Food Plants *Commelina*.

ACRAEA MIRANDA Riley
Desert Acraea
Identification Wingspan 5–5½cm. ♂
orange-red without black spots; pale and
black apical markings; dark marginal
band in hindwing: ♀ like ♂ but sometimes ochreous-grey not orange-red.
Range and Habitat Desert and arid bush
country from Somalia south to south-
eastern Ethiopia and Kenya. Flies close
to the ground amongst desert scrub, often
on sandy soil: extremely local but often
common in restricted habitat.

ACRAEA UVUI Grose-Smith
Tiny Acraea
Identification Wingspan 3½cm. One of the
smallest Acraeas, bright orange-brown with
extensive black marking but not spotted. Sexes
alike.
Range and Habitat High level forests, usually
over 5000 ft., in Angola, Cameroons, eastern
Congo, Uganda, Kenya and Tanzania (Kilimanjaro and Meru).

ACRAEA ACERATA Hewitson
Identification Wingspan 4cm. Variable, from
rich orange-brown to buffy-yellow; black border
broad and uniform; very small black patch at
extreme base of hindwing. *Acraea uvui* has a
more extensive black patch at base of hindwing.
Sexes alike.
Range and Habitat Ranges through most of the
Ethiopian Region north of South Africa. Found
in open bush and moorland, usually in vicinity of water. Flies throughout
the year.

ACRAEA EPONINA Cramer
Small Orange Acraea

Identification Wingspan 4cm. Bright orange-brown with orange-spotted black border. Sexes similar but ♀ more variable in colour and pattern. *Acraea ventura* has larger spots in the marginal bands and an orange apical patch on forewing.

Range and Habitat A very common species throughout most of the Ethiopian Region, found in a variety of habitats. Flies throughout the year.

Larval Food Plants *Hermannia, Triumfetta.*

♂   3cm

ACRAEA VENTURA Hewitson

Identification Wingspan 4cm. Bright orange-red with oval orange-red apical band; large wedge-shaped orange spots in fore and hindwing marginal bands. Sexes similar.

Range and Habitat Damp grasslands and marshy areas from Uganda and western Kenya south to Zambia. Local but not uncommon in favoured localities. Flies throughout the year.

♂   3cm

ACRAEA PHARSALUS Ward

Identification Wingspan 6–6½cm. ♂ forewing bright red with heavy black markings; narrow whitish apical bar; hindwing red with black spotting and black marginal border; some black suffusion in forewing of western race. ♀ resembles ♂ but duller and browner.

Range and Habitat Forests of West Africa, Congo to Uganda, Ethiopia and Kenya, south to Mozambique. Flies throughout the year.

♂

ACRAEA PERENNA Doubleday & Hewitson   p 96

Identification Wingspan 7½–8cm. Forewing very elongated, bright red, with or without some black suffusion; black markings and large apical patch;

hindwing with red spotted black marginal
band. ♀ averages larger and is usually
duller.
Range and Habitat A common forest
acraea found in West Africa, the Congo,
Ethiopia, Uganda, Kenya, Tanzania and
Malawi.

ACRAEA ORINA Hewitson
Identification Wingspan 5½–6cm. Forewing black with heavy bright red streaks;
hindwing bright red with black marginal
band and markings. Sexes alike.
Range and Habitat A West African forest
species ranging east through the Congo
to Uganda. Flies throughout the year.

ACRAEA PENELEOS Ward
Identification Wingspan 5½–6cm. ♂ forewing blackish, lightly scaled with transparent patches, some tinged red; hindwing brick red with black marginal band
and spotting. ♀ similar but usually larger
and duller.
Range and Habitat Forests of West Africa
and the Congo, east to Uganda, Ethiopia
and western Kenya. Flies throughout the
year.

ACRAEA PENELOPE Staudinger
Identification Wingspan 5–5½cm. ♂ forewing black with band of transparent
patches; hindwing red with black basal
area and marginal band. ♀ similar, but
in some the hindwing is yellow not red.
Range and Habitat A common West
African forest acraea which extends
across the Congo to Uganda and western
Kenya. Flies throughout the year.

♂   4cm

ACRAEA SERVONA Godart

Identification Wingspan $5\frac{1}{2}$–$6\frac{1}{2}$cm. Forewing blackish, lightly scaled, with whitish translucent patches; hindwing pale yellow with black marginal band and base. Sexes similar.

Range and Habitat Forests of West Africa from Nigeria to Angola, the Congo, Ethiopia, Uganda, Kenya and northern Tanzania. Flies throughout the year.

ACRAEA SEMIVITREA Aurivillius

p 96

Identification Wingspan $6\frac{1}{2}$–7cm. Forewing transparent with a black border; hindwing black at base and marginal band; large transparent area with yellow patch at hind angle of wing. Sexes alike.

Range and Habitat A forest species found in the Congo, Uganda and western Kenya. Flies throughout the year.

ACRAEA CINEREA Neave

Grey Acraea

Identification Wingspan 4–$4\frac{1}{2}$cm. Forewing transparent with lightly scaled grey apical patch; hindwing sooty grey, sometimes with a deep red patch. Sexes alike.

Range and Habitat Forests of Uganda and western Kenya: sometimes abundant, especially in Kalinzu Forest, south-western Uganda. Flies throughout the year.

 3cm

ACRAEA AMICITIAE Heron

Identification Wingspan 5–$5\frac{1}{2}$cm. Forewing bright chestnut-red with heavy black markings; a transparent apical bar; hindwing chestnut-red with heavily red-spotted marginal band. Sexes alike but some ♀♀ have red replaced by pale yellow.

Range and Habitat Mountain forests of Ruwenzori and Kigezi, Uganda; adjacent areas of Kivu, eastern Congo and Rwanda and Burundi. Flies throughout the year.

ACRAEA ALCIOPE Hewitson
Identification Wingspan 5½–6cm. ♂ forewing
black with a broad, curved median band orange-
yellow; hindwing orange-yellow with broad
black marginal band. ♀ variable, dark brown
with orange-brown bands; or dark brown with
orange-brown band on forewing, white band on
hindwing; or with forewing band orange, hindwing band orange-brown. In general appearance
this species is like a small *Bematistes*.

Range and Habitat A common forest species in
West Africa, the Congo, Uganda, western Kenya and Ethiopia.

ACRAEA JODUTTA Fabricius
Identification Wingspan 5½–6cm. ♂
forewing black with ochreous-yellow
subapical bar and patch; hindwing
black and ochreous-yellow. ♀ variable,
in typical form pale areas of fore and
hindwings white; or with subapical
bar yellowish-white and remainder of
pale markings orange-brown.

Range and Habitat A common forest
butterfly in West Africa, the Congo,
Uganda, western Kenya and Ethiopia. Flies throughout the year.

ACRAEA ESEBRIA Hewitson
Dusky Acraea
Identification Wingspan 5½–6cm. Variable: blackish with forewing subapical bar yellow to white and remainder of pale markings brownish-orange;
or the pale markings may be small and
greyish-yellow; or pale areas may be
orange brown, pale yellow or white.
Sexes similar.

Range and Habitat Common and widespread in forests, riverine thickets and
woodland from Angola and South Africa to Tanzania, Kenya and extreme
eastern Uganda. Flies throughout the year.
Larval Food Plants *Urera*, *Fleurya* and *Pouzolzia*.

ACRAEA LYCOA Godart

Identification Wingspan 5–5½cm. ♂ wings pale brown, lightly scaled, with indistinct pale spots on forewing; ♀ dark greyish-brown with indistinct pale spots on forewing and small white patch at base of hindwing. Race from northern Tanzania is blackish with yellow forewing spots in ♂, white in ♀.

♂

Range and Habitat Common forest species from West Africa to Ethiopia, Kenya and northern Tanzania. Flies throughout the year.

PARDOPSIS PUNCTATISSIMA Boisduval
Polka Dot

Identification Wingspan 4½cm. Pale yellowish-brown with black apical patch; covered evenly with round black dots; narrow black border to hindwing. Sexes alike.

Range and Habitat A dry bush country, savannah and open woodlands species found throughout the Ethiopian Region. Flies throughout the year.

♂   4cm

FAMILY NYMPHALIDAE
NYMPHALIDS

The Nymphalids are a very large family of medium or large-sized butterflies, many of which are robust and colourful. Some members of genera such as *Euxanthe*, *Charaxes*, *Salamis* and *Hypolimnas* are among the most beautiful of African insects.

A number of species exhibit striking sexual dimorphism, in which the ♂ and ♀ are quite dissimilar in colour; others are dimorphic in one or other sex; or they may exhibit extremes of seasonal dimorphism as in *Precis octavia*.

Characters of this family include greatly reduced forelegs; the hindwing cell is open or rarely partially closed by a very fine transverse vein; and the inner edge of the hindwing has a deep, curved groove to enclose the abdomen.
Early Stages. The eggs are laid, usually singly, on leaves of the food plant. The larvae are cylindrical, often with rows of spines and sometimes with spines on the head; in some, such as *Charaxes*, the body is smooth but head projections are present. The pupae are variously shaped, sometimes with metallic patches, and are attached by the tail.

EUXANTHE TRAJANUS Ward p 97
Identification Wingspan 9–10cm. The various species of *Euxanthe* are characterised by their large size, rounded wings and sailing, buoyant flight. ♂ forewing black with white markings and a chestnut-red patch at base; hindwing black with a large white or bluish-white patch and a row of white submarginal spots. ♀ usually larger with a more extensive white or yellowish hindwing patch. The similar *Euxanthe tiberius* ♂ has no white patch on hindwing.

Range and Habitat This is a rare West African and Congo forest butterfly which extends eastwards to Uganda. Flies high, often in semi-shade, but may be attracted to fermenting banana bait. Flies throughout the year.

EUXANTHE TIBERIUS Smith   p 97

Identification Wingspan 9–10cm. ♂
forewing black with bands of greenish-
white spots: submarginal spots white;
red-brown patch at base; hindwing
black with three white spots and row
of white marginal dots. ♀ resembles ♂
but forewing spots white, and large
white patch on hindwing.

Range and Habitat Eastern Kenya
west to Meru forests, Mt. Kenya, and
eastern Tanzania, inhabiting coastal
forests, woodland and dense thickets.
Flies in shady places and often remains
settled for long periods. Flight slow and buoyant, often high. On the wing
throughout the year.

Larval Food Plants *Deinbollia*.

EUXANTHE WAKEFIELDI Ward   p 97

Forest Queen

Identification Wingspan 7–9cm. ♂ velvety-black with semi-translucent
greenish-blue markings; ♀ with less rounded forewings than related species,
black with very pale bluish-white or white markings.

Range and Habitat Eastern Kenya, mainly coastal districts but extending
inland to Meru, Mt. Kenya, Tanzania, Mozambique, eastern border of
Rhodesia and northern Natal, South Africa. Inhabits coastal forests and
woodlands. Usually flies high, in semi-shade, but readily attracted to fermenting bananas. Flies throughout the year.

Larval Food Plants *Deinbollia*.

EUXANTHE EURINOME Cramer   p97
Identification Wingspan 8–9cm. ♂
velvety-black with pale blue markings; hindwing basal patch small: ♀
resembles ♂ but larger and bluish
markings paler. *Euxanthe crossleyi* has
larger hindwing patch and markings
are yellowish-green, not pale blue.
Range and Habitat A West African
and Congo forest species which extends eastwards to Uganda. Flies in

semi-shade in forest, but will come to fermenting bananas, and ♂♂ attracted
to leopard and civet droppings. Flies throughout the year.

EUXANTHE CROSSLEYI Ward   p97
Identification Wingspan 8–9½
cm. ♂ black with pale yellowish-
green markings; ♀ larger, blackish-brown, with more extensive
pale patch on hindwing. *Euxanthe eurinome* has less extensive hindwing patch and pale
markings are pale bluish-green,
not yellowish.
Range and Habitat West African
and Congo forests, eastwards
to Uganda and western Kenya.

Habits similar to related species. Flies throughout the year.

CHARAXES VARANES Cramer   p97
Pearl Charaxes
Identification Wingspan 7–8½cm. The Charaxes are medium to large-sized butterflies
with heavy bodies and triangular forewings:
hindwings with one, two, or more tails. Flight
strong and direct; attracted to fermenting
fruits, especially bananas, and ♂♂ feed on
animal droppings. *Charaxes varanes* is bright
reddish-brown with dark brown and pale
markings: basal half of both wings white
with a pearly sheen; single spatulate tail on

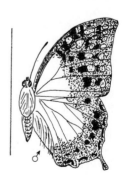

hindwing. Sexes similar, but ♀ usually larger. *Charaxes fulvescens* has straighter edge to forewing and white wing base strongly tinged yellow; dark markings less distinct.

Range and Habitat A common species throughout the Ethiopian Region, frequenting a variety of habitats from forest, woodland and savannah to bush country and gardens. Flies throughout the year.

Larval Food Plants *Allophyllus, Cardiospermum, Rhus, Schmidelia.*

CHARAXES FULVESCENS Aurivillius   p 97

Identification Wingspan 7½–8½cm. Forewing with straight outer margin; reddish-brown with dark brown and pale rufous markings, and large yellowish-white basal patch; single tail. Sexes similar, but ♀ usually larger. *Charaxes varanes* has pearly white basal patches.

Range and Habitat Forest areas, mainly low level, from West Africa and the Congo to Uganda, north-western Tanzania and western Kenya. A common species which flies throughout the year.

Larval Food Plants *Allophyllus.*

CHARAXES ACUMINATUS Thurau   p 97

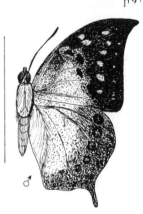

Identification Wingspan 8–9cm. Forewing, apex sharply pointed and tapering and outer margin concave; dark orange-brown with ochreous-orange spots and dark brown markings; pale orange-rufous to pearly white at base; single tail. Sexes alike, but ♀ usually larger. *Charaxes fulvescens* lacks pointed apex to forewing and outer margin straight, not strongly concave.

Range and Habitat High level and mountain forest in Uganda, Kenya and Tanzania to Zambia, Malawi and eastern Rhodesia. Flies throughout the year.

CHARAXES CANDIOPE Godart p 97
Green-veined Charaxes

Identification Wingspan 7–9cm. ♂ bright orange-yellow, paler towards base of wings, with blackish-brown markings; main veins of forewing green; two tails on hindwing. Sexes similar, but ♀ larger and with longer tails; outer margin of forewing concave.

Range and Habitat A common species throughout most of the Ethiopian Region; inhabits forest, woodland, savannah and bush country. Flies throughout the year.

Larval Food Plants Croton.

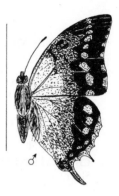

CHARAXES PROTOCLEA Feisthamel p 112
Flame-bordered Charaxes

Identification Wingspan 7–9cm. ♂ velvety-black, with an orange-red patch on hind angle of forewing and broad fiery orange-red band on hindwing: ♀ blackish-brown, with broad white band on fore and hindwing; narrow orange-red marginal band on hindwing. ♂ with one very short tail; ♀ with two short tails. The eastern and southern race, *azota*, has a broad orange-red marginal band on forewing in the ♂; the ♀ has a band of orange spots on forewing.

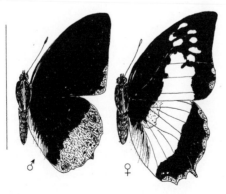

NYMPHALIDAE – CHARAXES

1 **CHARAXES VIOLETTA** ♂ ♀   *page* 136
   White transverse stripe on underside.

2 **CHARAXES SMARAGDALIS** ♂ ♀   138
   Hindwing mainly blue.

3 **CHARAXES CITHAERON** ♂ ♀   138
   No white transverse stripe on underside.

4 **CHARAXES NUMENIUS** ♂ ♀   137
   Short tails: thin white line across underside.

5 **CHARAXES BIPUNCTATUS** ♂ ♀   139
   Tails very short or absent: no thin white line on underside.

6 **CHARAXES BOHEMANI** ♂ ♀   137
   Basal areas fore and hindwings extensively blue.

1 ♀ ♂
2 ♂
2 ♀
3 ♀ 3 ♀
4 ♂ 4 ♀
5 ♂
6 ♂ 6 ♀
5 ♀

1 ♂   1 ♀   2 ♀   2 ♂   3   4 ♂   4 ♀   5 ♂   5 ♀   6 ♂   6 ♀   7 ♀   7 ♂

PLATE 14   129

NYMPHALIDAE – CHARAXES

1 **CHARAXES TIRIDATES** ♂ ♀   *page* 138
   Orange marginal streaks on hindwing.

2 **CHARAXES MIXTUS** ♂ ♀   139
   Bluish marginal streaks on hindwing.

3 **CHARAXES PYTHODORUS** ♂   142
   Sexes similar but ♀ larger: tailless.

4 **CHARAXES JAHLUSA** ♂ ♀   147

5 **CHARAXES NANDINA** ♂ ♀   140
   Usually with long tails.

6 **CHARAXES AMELIAE** ♂ ♀   141
   ♂ heavy blue submarginal spots.

7 **CHARAXES XIPHARES** ♂ ♀   140
   Usually short thick tails.

Range and Habitat Occurs in low level forest and woodland throughout tropical Africa, south to Mozambique, Malawi and Rhodesia. Flies throughout the year.
Larval Food Plants *Afzelia, Syzygium.*

CHARAXES BOUETI Feisthamel p 112
Red Forest Charaxes
Identification Wingspan 6½–8cm. ♂ orange-brown with blackish-brown markings; hindwing orange-brown with submarginal band; underside yellowish-buff with reddish median line bordered yellowish-white: two tails; ♀ paler, with yellowish band on forewing, breaking into spots on apex. The very similar *Charaxes lasti* has a slender silvery band across underside of hindwing. The race of *Charaxes boueti* which inhabits high mountain forest of south-western Uganda – *C. b. alticola* – is very distinct with a white band on the hindwing.

Range and Habitat Occurs in both savannah woodland and high altitude forest in Nigeria eastwards to southern Sudan and Ethiopia, south through eastern Kenya, south-western Uganda and Tanzania to Mozambique, Malawi, Zambia, Rhodesia and southern Congo. Flies throughout the year.
Larval Food Plants *Oxytenanthera* (bamboo).

CHARAXES LASTI Grose-Smith p 112
Silver-striped Charaxes
Identification Wingspan 6½–7½cm. ♂ bright orange-red with black marginal markings; underside with silvery-white line down centre of hindwing; two tails. ♀ larger and paler, with longer tails. The race of *Charaxes boueti* which occurs alongside *Charaxes lasti* has a wider yellowish band down centre of hindwing underside.

Range and Habitat Coastal forests and woodland in eastern Kenya and eastern Tanzania. Locally common, as in Sokoke–Arabuku Forest, Kenya coast. Flies throughout the year.
Larval Food Plants *Afzelia.*

CHARAXES CYNTHIA Butler p112
Western Red Charaxes

Identification Wingspan 6½–7½cm. ♂ black with bright orange-brown markings; two short tails; underside with narrow silvery band down centre of hindwing. ♀ larger with a pale buffy-yellow band on fore and hindwing. *Charaxes lucretius* ♂ has a purplish-violet iridescence on upper surface and both sexes lack silvery bar on underside of hindwing.

Range and Habitat A common forest charaxes in West Africa, the Congo, Uganda and western Kenya. Flies throughout the year.

CHARAXES LUCRETIUS Cramer p112
Violet-washed Charaxes

Identification Wingspan 6½–7½cm. ♂ deep black with bright red-brown markings; distinct purplish-violet iridescence over upper surface of wings in certain lights; underside brick-red without silvery bar on hindwing; two very short tails. ♀ with yellowish-white band across fore and hindwings; two short tails, slightly longer than in ♂.

Range and Habitat Forests of West Africa and the Congo, eastwards to Uganda and western Kenya. Flies throughout the year.

CHARAXES LACTITINCTUS Karsch p112
Blue-patch Charaxes

Identification Wingspan 6–7½cm. ♂ black with orange-red markings, often with a purplish sheen, and a bluish-white basal patch on both fore and hindwings; two tails. ♀ larger and paler with more extensive orange-red markings.

Range and Habitat An inhabitant of savannah woodland and bush country from West Africa across northern

Congo to southern Sudan, northern Uganda, southern Ethiopia and north-
western Kenya. Uncommon and local species. Flies throughout the year.
Larval Food Plants *Syzygium cordatum*.

CHARAXES JASIUS   p 113
Foxy Charaxes

Identification Wingspan 7½–9½cm. Two very distinct races of the European
Charaxes jasius occur in Africa – *C. j. epijasius* in the north and west,
C. j. saturnus in the east and south. The former is dark purplish-brown with
broad orange-yellow marginal bands; hindwing with bright pale blue submarginal patch; two tails. *C. j. saturnus* is red-brown with outer area black,
and an orange-brown median band; marginal row of orange spots on hindwing, and submarginal row of blue spots. Sexes alike, but ♀ larger with longer
tails.

Range and Habitat Savannah country, woodlands and bush throughout the
Ethiopian Region. *C. j. saturnus* occurs from eastern Kenya to Malawi,
Mozambique, Zambia, southern Congo, Rhodesia and South Africa; *C. j.
epijasius* to west and north of this range. Flies throughout the year.

Larval Food Plants *Afzelia, Bauhinia, Brachystegia* and *Hibiscus*.

C. j. epijasius   *C. j. saturnus*

CHARAXES PELIAS Cramer   p 113
Protea Charaxes

Identification Wingspan 6–7cm. This species is very similar to *Charaxes jasius
saturnus*, but tails are shorter and thicker and apex of forewing is less acute;

underside mainly grey with basal streaks maroon. In *C. j. saturnus* the ground colour of underside is pale reddish-brown with grey streaks. Sexes similar but ♀ larger.

Range and Habitat A very local species confined to mountains of Western Cape, South Africa, where associated with Protea bushes. Flies from September to April.

Larval Food Plants *Bauhinia, Rafnia, Schotia, Hypocalyptus.*

CHARAXES HANSALI

p 113

Cream-banded Charaxes

Identification Wingspan 7–8½cm. ♂ blackish-grey, paler and browner towards base with yellowish-white median band; two tails. Sexes alike, but ♀ larger and with longer tails.

Range and Habitat Somalia, Ethiopia, northern Uganda and Kenya. Inhabits scrub-covered hills, arid bush country and open savannah woodland: local and uncommon. Flies throughout the year.

Larval Food Plants *Salvadora persica, Osyris.*

CHARAXES CASTOR Cramer

p 113

Giant Charaxes

Identification Wingspan 8–11cm. ♂ dark brown with pale ochreous-orange median band (creamy-yellow in eastern and southern race); hindwing with blue marginal and submarginal spots; two long slender tails. ♀ resembles ♂ but larger and with longer tails.

Range and Habitat Forests of tropical Africa, south to northern South Africa. Inhabits forest, wooded areas, coastal scrub and bush country. Flies throughout the year.

Larval Food Plants *Afzelia, Sorghum, Tragia* and *Gymnosporia.*

CHARAXES BRUTUS Cramer
White-barred Charaxes
Identification Wingspan 7½–9cm. ♂
blackish with white or creamy-white
median band; two tails. Sexes similar,
but ♀ larger with slightly more rounded
wings and longer tails.
Range and Habitat A common species
in forests and wooded areas throughout the Ethiopian Region. Flies
throughout the year.
Larval Food Plants *Ekebergia*, *Grewia*,
Turraea, *Trichilia* and *Melia*.

p 112

CHARAXES ANSORGEI Rothschild
Ansorge's Charaxes
Identification Wingspan 7–8½cm. ♂
forewing blackish-brown merging to
dark chestnut-brown towards base,
with black markings and a yellowish-
orange band; hindwing blackish with
a mauve-white band and orange submarginal spots; two tails. ♀ larger with
a white median band (orange-white in
some races) on forewing; tails longer.
Range and Habitat Highland forest in
Kenya, Uganda and Tanzania: uncommon and local. Flies throughout
the year.
Larval Food Plants *Bersama abyssinica*.

p 113

CHARAXES POLLUX Cramer
Black-bordered Charaxes
Identification Wingspan 7–8½cm. ♂
rich orange-brown with a broad
orange-yellow median band and black
costal markings on forewing; broad
black margin to both fore and hindwings; three tails; hindwing above
tails deeply serrated. ♀ larger with

p 112

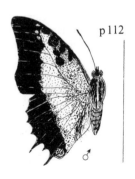

longer tails. Eastern and southern race with orange marginal spots.

Range and Habitat A locally common species throughout tropical Africa, south to Mozambique and Rhodesia. Inhabits forest, woodland and lush coastal scrub. Flies throughout the year.

Larval Food Plants *Bersama*, *Sorindeia*.

CHARAXES PHOEBUS Butler   p 113
Abyssinian Charaxes

Identification Wingspan 7–8½cm. ♂ rufous-brown with a yellowish-brown median band; black submarginal band on fore and hindwings, with a marginal yellow border; two tails. ♀ like ♂ but larger, a paler median band and longer tails.

Range and Habitat Highland forest and wooded areas of Ethiopian highlands: local and uncommon. Flies throughout the year.

CHARAXES DRUCEANUS Butler   p 113
Silver-barred Charaxes

Identification Wingspan 8–10cm. ♂ bright red-brown with black markings and a broad black submarginal band on both wings; orange marginal spots on forewing, a narrow marginal band on hindwing; two tails. ♀ resembles ♂ but paler and with longer tails. Underside in both sexes marked with broad silver bands and stripes.

Range and Habitat Forest areas, usually high level, in Nigeria, the Cameroons and Gabon in West Africa; Kenya, Uganda, Kivu Province, Congo, Rwanda and Burundi, south to Zambia, Rhodesia and South Africa. Flies throughout the year.

Larval Food Plants *Eugenia*, *Syzygium*.

CHARAXES EUDOXUS Drury

p 113

Identification Wingspan 7–8cm. ♂ forewing black with reddish-brown patch at base; narrow orange-brown median band and orange marginal spots; hindwing reddish-brown with black submarginal band; brown patch at base; two tails. ♀ larger, with pale yellowish-brown median band; tails longer.

Range and Habitat West Africa to the Congo, Uganda and western Kenya. Inhabits forested areas and heavy riverine woodland. Flies throughout the year.

Larval Food Plants *Syzygium*.

CHARAXES VIOLETTA Grose-Smith
Violet-spotted Charaxes

p 128

Identification Wingspan 6½–8cm. ♂ forewing black with violet-blue median band and spots; hindwing black with broad violet-blue median band shading to white towards inner margin; submarginal blue spots; two tails; underside with straight white band down centre of hindwing. ♀ forewing black with solid white median band; white spots in apex; hindwing blackish-brown with broad, violet-tinged white band and whitish submarginal spots; tails longer than ♂. *Charaxes cithaeron* (♂ and ♀) closely resembles this species but is bluer and there is no white line on underside of hindwing.

Range and Habitat Forests and heavy woodland of eastern Kenya, Tanzania, Mozambique, Malawi, Rhodesia and Natal, South Africa. Flies throughout the year.

Larval Food Plants *Deinbollia*.

CHARAXES NUMENIUS Hewitson p 128

Identification Wingspan 7–8½cm. ♂ black with a strong blue sheen; fore and hind-wings with marginal orange spots; two rows of small blue spots in forewing and hindwing; two very short tails. ♀ fore-wing olive-brown with black apical patch and two apical white spots; white median band; hindwing olive-brown with blue-spotted black marginal band. Underside of hindwing in both sexes with dark band edged white, which distinguishes this species from the closely related *Charaxes tiridates* and *Charaxes bipunctatus*.

Range and Habitat Forest areas of West Africa, the Congo, east to Ethiopia, Uganda, western Kenya and western Tanzania. Flies throughout the year.

Larval Food Plants *Erythrina*, *Grewia*, *Allophylus*, *Deinbollia* and *Phialodiscus zambesiacus*.

CHARAXES BOHEMANI Felder p 128
Large Blue Charaxes

Identification Wingspan 7½–8½cm. ♂ basal half of forewing and most of hindwing bright pale blue; remainder black with two apical white spots on forewing and bluish submarginal spots on hindwing; two tails. ♀ larger with a white discal band on forewing.

Range and Habitat South-eastern Kenya, Tanzania, Mozambique, Zambia, Malawi, southern Congo and Rhodesia to Transvaal, South Africa. Frequents woodlands and coastal bush, especially Brachystegia woodland. Flies throughout the year.

Larval Food Plants *Afzelia*.

CHARAXES CITHAERON Felder   p 128
Blue-spotted Charaxes

Identification Wingspan 7½–9cm. ♂ forewing black with blue band and spots; hindwing black with large pale blue patch shading to whitish on inner side; two tails. ♀ blackish-brown with white forewing band and bluish-white patch on hindwing. *Charaxes violetta* differs in having violet-blue markings in ♂ and white stripe down underside of hindwing.

Range and Habitat Kenya, southwards through Tanzania to Mozambique, Malawi, Zambia, Rhodesia and South Africa. Inhabits forested and wooded areas. Flies throughout the year.

Larval Food Plants *Afzelia*, *Albizia*, *Baphia*, *Craibia*, *Cola*, *Chaetacme* and *Trema*.

CHARAXES SMARAGDALIS Butler   p 128
Western Blue Charaxes

Identification Wingspan 7½–9cm. ♂ forewing bluish-black with bright blue median band and spots; hindwing bright blue with black basal area and narrow black marginal band enclosing blue spots; two short tails. ♀ larger, with very broad white (in some races blue) median band on forewing. Blue deeper than *Charaxes cithaeron* and *Charaxes violetta* and more extensive on hindwing.

Range and Habitat A forest species found in West Africa, the Congo and eastwards to Uganda, western Kenya and western Tanzania. Flies throughout the year.

Larval Food Plants ? *Grewia*.

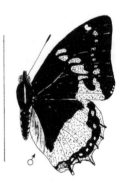

CHARAXES TIRIDATES Cramer   p 129
Identification Wingspan 8–10cm. ♂ bluish-black with orange marginal spots and

round blue spots on fore and hindwings; two tails. ♀ olive-brown with a black apical patch, a broken white forewing band and two white spots near apex; hindwing with submarginal black border enclosing blue spots; tails longer than in ♂ and insect larger. The rare *Charaxes mixtus* ♂ has bluish marginal spots on hindwing, the ♀ is bluish-grey and black, not olive-brown. *Charaxes numenes* has dark bar edged with white on underside of hindwing. *Charaxes bipunctatus* lacks distinct tails.

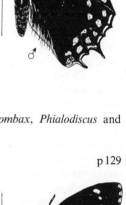

Range and Habitat A common forest charaxes from West Africa and the Congo to Ethiopia, Uganda, western Kenya and western Tanzania. Flies throughout the year.

Larval Food Plants *Grewia, Hibiscus, Albizia, Bombax, Phialodiscus* and *Osyris*.

CHARAXES MIXTUS Rothschild   p 129

Identification Wingspan 8–10cm. ♂ apical half of forewing black, blue-black towards base; median and submarginal bands of bluish-white spots; two white spots in apex; marginal spots buff-white; hindwing bluish-black with two rows of submarginal bluish-white spots; marginal streaks bluish, not orange as in *Charaxes tiridates* and related species; two short tails. ♀ resembles ♂ but larger and upper tail longer; blue spots larger.

Range and Habitat A rare forest species recorded from the Cameroons and the Congo. Flies throughout the year.

CHARAXES BIPUNCTATUS Rothschild   p 128

Identification Wingspan 7½–9½cm. ♂ bright blue-black or violet-black with a few scattered blue spots; marginal spots orange; two tails barely indicated. ♀ olive-brown with apical half of forewing black, with white median band

and two white spots in apex; hindwing with narrow black submarginal border enclosing blue dots; marginal spots yellowish-olive; tails barely indicated, about ½mm. long. *Charaxes tiridates* can always be distinguished by its longer tails.
Range and Habitat A West African forest species which ranges across the Congo to Uganda and western Kenya. Flies throughout the year.

p 129

CHARAXES XIPHARES Cramer
Forest King Charaxes
Identification Wingspan 7–9cm. ♂ bluish-black with heavy bright blue markings on forewing and a thick vivid blue band on hindwing; two tails relatively short and thick. ♀ blackish-brown with relatively short white median band on forewing and two white spots in apex; patch on hindwing either yellowish or white; tail short and thick. Other races of this species from northern Tanzania and Mt. Kulal, northern Kenya, differ in having long tails.
Range and Habitat Forested areas of South Africa, north to eastern Rhodesia, Malawi, Tanzania, south-western Uganda

and Mt. Kulal, northern Kenya. Uncommon and local. In South Africa flies from October to April/May: elsewhere throughout the year.
Larval Food Plants *Cryptocarya*.

CHARAXES NANDINA Rothschild   p 129
Identification Wingspan 8–9½cm. ♂ bluish-black with a blue patch on the hind margin of the forewing and bluish-white spotting forming two narrow bands across the wing; hindwing with narrow discal blue patch, a row of post-discal spots and a line of submarginal blue dots; marginal markings of fore and hindwings yellowish-orange; two tails. ♀ blackish-brown with short broken median band and band of post-discal spots white; hindwing with ochreous patch. Similar in general appearance to some of the South African races of

Charaxes xiphares but ♂ distinguished by presence of blue post-discal spots on hindwing and pattern of ♀ also different.

Range and Habitat A local and uncommon species found only in the eastern highlands of Kenya (Mt. Kenya, Aberdare Mts., Kikuyu and Nairobi district). Flies throughout the year but most frequent during and after rains.

Larval Food Plants *Drypetes gerrardii*, *Craibia*, and *Hippocrates obtusifolia*.

CHARAXES AMELIAE Doumet   p 129

Identification Wingspan $7\frac{1}{2}$–$9\frac{1}{2}$cm. ♂ iridescent bluish-black with brilliant large blue spots; two short tails. ♀ dark brown merging to olive-brown at base with white or pale ochreous spots on forewing; hindwing with white median band and bluish-white submarginal spots; narrow orange-white margin. Underside silvery in both sexes.

Range and Habitat A relatively common forest species found in West Africa and the Congo, east to Uganda, western Kenya, western Tanzania and Malawi. Flies throughout the year.

CHARAXES IMPERIALIS Butler   p 144

Identification Wingspan 7–9cm. ♂ blue-black with a blue band across fore and hindwing; bluish-white spots below costa of forewing; two tails. ♀ dark bluish-brown with yellowish or white spots on forewing, and a blue band on fore and hindwings; underside pale olive-grey with some dark markings.

Range and Habitat An uncommon and local forest species found in West Africa, the Congo and Uganda, where most frequent in western forests. Flies throughout the year.

CHARAXES PYTHODORUS Hewitson  p 129
Identification Wingspan 7–8½cm. ♂
bluish-black with very broad bluish-
white band across both wings; bluish-
white spots on forewing; no tails;
underside pale greenish-grey with indistinct markings. ♀ similar but larger.
Range and Habitat A local and uncommon forest and woodland species
found in West Africa and the Congo
east to Uganda, Kenya, Tanzania and
Zambia. Flies throughout the year. **Larval Food Plants** *Craibia*.

CHARAXES HADRIANUS Ward   p 144
Identification Wingspan 8½–9½cm. ♂
apical half of forewing black with
yellowish-white spots; basal patch red-
brown; very broad median band
yellowish-white; hindwing yellowish-
white with brown submarginal spots
and small red-brown basal patch; two
tails. Sexes similar, but ♀ larger.
Underside whitish with red-brown
streak down centre of hindwing.
Range and Habitat A rare forest species
recorded from West Africa and the
Congo; one record from Katera
Forest, Uganda. Flies throughout the year.

CHARAXES NOBILIS Druce   p 144
Identification Wingspan 8½–10cm. ♂
black with very broad yellow band
across fore and hindwing; black marginal band on hindwing enclosing blue
spots; two tails; underside silvery-
white with black lines. ♀ similar, but
larger and forewing apex rounder.
Range and Habitat A very uncommon
West African and Congo forest
species; recorded also in Kalinzu Forest, western Uganda. Flies throughout
the year.

CHARAXES FOURNIERAE Le Moult   p 144

Identification Wingspan 9–11½cm. ♂ velvety-black with two large golden-orange patches on forewing and large golden-orange patch on hindwing: apex of forewing elongated and outer margin of wing deeply concave; no tails but margin of hindwing deeply incised above anal angle. ♀ similar to ♂ but larger and with longer, more rounded wings.

Range and Habitat High level forest of south-western Kigezi, Uganda (Impenetrable-Kayonza Forest) and in the French Cameroons.

CHARAXES ACRAEOIDES Druce   p 144

Identification Wingspan 8½–9cm. ♂ black with a short white bar in the forewing apex and a large pinkish-red patch on inner margin of forewing; hindwing pinkish-red with a black marginal band: apex of forewing elongated and outer margin of forewing deeply concave; no tails but hindwing deeply incised above anal margin. ♀ not examined.

Range and Habitat A rare forest species known only from the French Cameroons and the French Congo.

CHARAXES KAHLDENI Homeyer & Dewitz   p 144

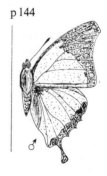

Identification Wingspan 5½–6½cm. ♂ greenish-white with an opalescent tint; apex and margin of forewing orange-brown with yellowish spots; hindwing with narrow orange-brown marginal border; one spatulate tail. ♀ larger and has two spatulate tails.

Range and Habitat West Africa from the Cameroons to Angola, eastwards through the Congo and western Uganda (Bwamba Forest). Flies throughout the year.

NYMPHALIDAE – CHARAXES

1 **CHARAXES ZOOLINA** ♂ws ♀ws ♂ds ♀ds   *page* 146
Spatulate tails.

2 **CHARAXES KAHLDENI** ♂   143
♀ with two tails: spatulate tails.

3 **CHARAXES ZINGHA** ♂ ♀   148
Lobed hindwings.

4 **CHARAXES EUPALE** ♂   146
Sexes similar but ♀ larger: green apical patch extends to inner edge of
forewing.

5 **CHARAXES DILUTUS** ♂   147
Sexes similar but ♀ larger: green apical patch more restricted not
extending to inner edge of forewing.

6 **CHARAXES FOURNIERAE** ♂   143
♀ larger and with rounder wings: golden apical patch.

7 **CHARAXES ACRAEOIDES** ♂   143
White apical patch.

8 **CHARAXES NOBILIS** ♂   142
Sexes similar but ♀ larger and with longer tails: broad yellow bands.

9 **CHARAXES IMPERIALIS** ♂ ♀   141
Blue hindwing band.

10 **CHARAXES HADRIANUS** ♂   142
Sexes similar but ♀ larger: hindwing mainly creamy-yellow.

1 ♂ ws   1 ♀ ws   1 ♂ ds   1 ♀ ds   2

3 ♂   3 ♀   4   5

6   7   8

9 ♂   9 ♀   10

1 ♂ 1 ♀ 2 3 ♂ 3 ♀

4 ♀ 5 ♂ 5 ♀

4 ♂

7 ♂ 7 ♀

6 8 ♂ 8 ♀ 9

10 ♂ 10 ♀ 11 ♂ 11 ♀

PLATE 16   145

NYMPHALIDAE – CHARAXES

1 **CHARAXES BLANDA** ♂ ♀   *page* 151
Serrated wing margins.

2 **CHARAXES HILDEBRANDTI** ♂   151
Sexes similar but ♀ larger: blue-edged white band.

3 **CHARAXES ANTICLEA** ♂ ♀   150
♂ black spots on red hindwing patch: ♀ broad orange-brown band.

4 **CHARAXES ACHAEMENES** ♂ ♀   149
♂ white band: ♀ resembles *Charaxes jasius saturnus* but underside
quite different: see text.

5 **CHARAXES OPINATUS** ♂ ♀   150
Red hindwing margin.

6 **CHARAXES THYSI** ♂   151
Violet-blue band.

7 **CHARAXES PAPHIANUS** ♂ ♀   148
Sharply attenuated forewing tip.

8 **CHARAXES PLEIONE** ♂ ♀   147
Forewing tip not attenuated.

9 **CHARAXES PENRICEI** ♂   149
Sexes similar: ♀ very like ♀ *Charaxes etesipe tavetensis*: see text.

10 **CHARAXES ETESIPE ETESIPE** ♂ ♀   148
♂ blue spots on hindwing: ♀ relatively narrow white or cream band.

11 **CHARAXES ETESIPE TAVETENSIS** ♂ ♀   148
♂ blue patch on hindwing: ♀ relatively broad white or cream band.

CHARAXES ZOOLINA Westwood p 144
Club-tailed Charaxes

Identification Wingspan 4½–6cm. Species remarkable in having distinct wet and dry season forms. Wet season ♂ greenish-white with broad blackish-brown border enclosing greenish-white spots; one spatulate tail. ♀ is larger and has two spatulate tails and larger spots in marginal band. Dry season ♂ pale orange-brown with reddish-brown border; one spatulate tail. ♀ larger with two tails. Intermediates between these seasonal forms recorded but very uncommon.

Range and Habitat Forest, woodland, savannah country and bush from Ethiopia south through Kenya and Uganda to Rhodesia and South Africa: common. Flies throughout the year.

Larval Food Plants *Acacia pennata*.

CHARAXES EUPALE Drury p 144

Identification Wingspan 4½–5½cm. ♂ bright greenish-cream with an opalescent sheen; apical patch olive-green, extending down outer edge of forewing and along the hind margin for a short distance; olive-green spot in cell of forewing; hindwing with brownish-olive marginal spots; no tails. ♀ similar to ♂ but larger. Underside green with few silvery markings. The very similar *Charaxes dilutus* has a paler and less extensive green apex, which does not reach the inner margin; the spot in the forewing cell is usually absent and underside silvery markings are more extensive.

Range and Habitat A common forest species in West Africa and the Congo, east to Uganda, Kenya and western Tanzania. Flies throughout the year. Although an abundant insect in many places, the ♀ is seldom encountered and is rare in collections.

Larval Food Plants *Scutia* and *Albizia*.

CHARAXES DILUTUS Rothschild

p 144

Identification Wingspan 4½–5½cm. ♂ bright greenish-cream with an opalescent sheen; apical patch pale green, paler and less extensive than in *Charaxes eupale*; small dark submarginal spots on hindwing; underside with silvery markings well developed. ♀ like ♂ but larger and paler.

Range and Habitat Forest areas of West Africa and the Congo, to Uganda and Kenya. Flies throughout the year.

Larval Food Plants *Scutia.*

3cm ♂

CHARAXES JAHLUSA Trimen

p 129

Pearl-spotted Charaxes

Identification Wingspan 4–5½cm. ♂ bright red-brown with black spots and a red-spotted marginal band; two tails. ♀ larger, pale orange-brown; wings rounder, forewing less concave than in ♂.

Range and Habitat Ethiopia southwards through Kenya and eastern Uganda to Mozambique, Rhodesia and South Africa.

Larval Food Plants *Grewia.*

3cm ♂

CHARAXES PLEIONE Godart

p 145

Identification Wingspan 4½–5½cm. ♂ bright orange-brown with blackish-brown apex and markings; two short tails. ♀ larger and paler with more clearly defined markings. Forewing apex not strongly attenuated.

Range and Habitat A forest species common in West Africa and the Congo, east to Uganda, Tanzania and western Kenya. Flies throughout the year.

3cm ♂

CHARAXES PAPHIANUS Ward p 145

Identification Wingspan 4½–5cm. ♂ forewing apex very pointed and attenuated; orange-brown with dark brown markings; one thick tail. ♀ larger and paler. The related *Charaxes pleione* lacks the attenuated forewing apex and has two tails, not one.

Range and Habitat Forests from West Africa and the Congo to Uganda and western Kenya. Flies throughout the year.

Larval Food Plants Various climbing Acacias.

3cm ♂

CHARAXES ZINGHA Stoll p 144

Identification Wingspan 6½–8cm. ♂ bright pinkish-red with very broad black borders; red spots in border of hindwing; no tails but anal angle projects in the form of a rounded protuberance. ♀ larger and paler, orange-red not bright pinkish-red.

Range and Habitat Forests of West Africa and the Congo, east to Uganda: uncommon and local. Flies throughout the year.

Larval Food Plants *Hugonia platysepala*.

♂

CHARAXES ETESIPE Godart p 145

Identification Wingspan 6½–7½cm. ♂ forewing bluish-black with blue and white spots: hindwing with row of post-discal large blue spots and a submarginal row of white spots; two tails: underside cream with grey suffusion, marked with black and chestnut. ♀ blackish-brown with median band white or ochreous-yellow. The eastern and southern race, *C. e. tavetensis* has a blue patch on the hindwing in the ♂; the ♀ is dark olive-brown usually with a pale ochreous median band.

Range and Habitat Forests and wooded areas from West Africa and the Congo,

♂

east to Ethiopia and Kenya, south to eastern border of Rhodesia and Mozambique. *C. e. tavetensis* occurs in eastern Kenya southwards to Rhodesia and Mozambique. Flies throughout the year.

Larval Food Plants *Ricinus* (Castor Oil plant), *Afzelia*, *Dalbergia*, *Cassia*, *Entada scadens*, *Entada gigas*, and *Entada abyssinicus*.

CHARAXES PENRICEI Rothschild   p 145

Identification Wingspan 6–7cm. ♂ blue-black with a greenish sheen at base; large white spots and a short white band on forewing; bluish-white median band and row of whitish submarginal spots on hindwings; two tails. Some specimens have white markings suffused blue. ♀ similar to ♂ but larger and with longer tails. This sex is very like ♀ *Charaxes etesipe tavetensis* but may be distinguished by underside pattern and colour, the hind-wing costal and subcostal pale markings being white, not cream; and the oblique white bar on the forewing is nearer to the base than in *C. e. tavetensis*.

Range and Habitat An uncommon and local species found mainly in Bra-chystegia woodland in Tanzania, Malawi, Zambia, Rhodesia and Angola.

CHARAXES ACHAEMENES Felder   p 145
Bush Charaxes

Identification Wingspan 7–8½cm. ♂ fore-wing attenuated, blackish-brown merging to olive-brown towards base; white median band across fore and hindwings; row of bluish-white submarginal spots on hindwing; two tails; undersurface resembles that of *Charaxes etesipe*. ♀ dark brown to reddish-brown towards base; pale orange-brown median band; blue submarginal spots on hindwing; two long tails. ♀ resembles *Charaxes jasius saturnus* above, but underside similar to that of *Charaxes etesipe*.

Range and Habitat A woodland and bush country species throughout most of the Ethiopian Region, including South Africa. In South Africa flies from September to April; elsewhere on the wing throughout the year.

CHARAXES ANTICLEA Drury

p 145

Identification Wingspan 6–6½cm. ♂ black-ish-brown to black with orange-red patch near base of forewing margin, and a broad marginal orange-red band on hindwing containing row of submarginal black spots; two short tails. ♀ brown with very broad pale orange-brown median band: tails longer.

Range and Habitat Forests of West Africa and the Congo to Uganda, western Tanzania and western Kenya. Flies throughout the year.

Larval Food Plants *Acacia pennata* and *Acacia goetzi*.

CHARAXES OPINATUS Heron

p 145

Identification Wingspan 5½–6½cm. ♂ forewing dark brown without markings; hindwing dark brown with narrow brick-red marginal band and row of bluish-white submarginal spots; two tails. ♀ resembles ♂ but with narrow white median band.

Range and Habitat A rare mountain forest species known from the Ruwenzori Mts., and highland forest in south-western Kigezi, Uganda. Flies throughout the year.

CHARAXES BAUMANNI Rogenhofer

p 113

Identification Wingspan 4½–6cm. ♂ black with short pale blue band and bluish-white spots on forewing; blue median band on hindwing; two tails. ♀ blackish-brown with white median band and spots.

Range and Habitat A woodland, forest and dense bush species found in East Africa south to Malawi and Rhodesia. Flies throughout the year.

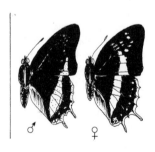

Larval Food Plants *Acacia pennata, Pterilobium lacerans.*

CHARAXES THYSI Capronnier   p145
Identification Wingspan 5–6cm. ♂ black
with a bright violet-blue median band
across both wings; blue marginal spots
on hindwing; two tails. ♀ not examined.
Range and Habitat A rare forest species
known only from the southern Congo
(Kassai).

CHARAXES HILDEBRANDTI Dewitz   p145
Identification Wingspan 6–7cm. ♂ black
with white median band edged with pale
blue; two short tails. Sexes similar but ♀
larger and with longer tails.
Range and Habitat An uncommon and
local forest species found in West Africa,
the Congo and western Uganda (Bwamba
Forest, Toro).

CHARAXES BLANDA Rothschild   p145
Identification Wingspan 6–7cm. ♂ forewing attenuated and wing margins serrated; blue-black with greenish tinge
towards base; bluish-white spots and blue
patch on forewing; hindwing with large
greenish-blue patch; black marginal
border with bluish-white spots; two tails.
♀ resembles ♂ but larger and with longer
tails.
Range and Habitat An uncommon and
local species found in Brachystegia woodlands of eastern Kenya and eastern Tanzania: most frequent in Sokoke–Arabuku
Forest, Kenya coast. Flies throughout
the year.
Larval Food Plants *Brachystegia*.

CHARAXES GUDERIANA Dewitz   p160
Blue-spangled Charaxes
Identification Wingspan 5½–7cm. Forewing attenuated and margin concave;

♂ bluish-black; white and bluish-white spots and white marginal spots on forewing; thick blue post-discal band and row of white submarginal spots on hindwing; two tails. ♀ blackish-brown to red-brown towards base with pale orange-brown median band and spots. *Charaxes gallagheri* ♂ differs in having a white patch on the hindwing costa and underside silvery-white, whilst ♀ has white median band.

Range and Habitat Brachystegia woodlands from eastern Kenya south through Tanzania, Malawi, Rhodesia and Angola. Flies throughout the year.

Larval Food Plants *Brachystegia.*

CHARAXES GALLAGHERI van Son
Gallagher's Charaxes
Identification Wingspan 5–7 cm. ♂ bluish-black with white and bluish spots on forewing; square white spot on costa of hindwing; a narrow greenish-blue band and a row of white submarginal spots; two tails; underside silvery-white with dark markings. ♀ blackish-brown with white median band and spots: similar to

Charaxes ethalion but underside silvery-white, not reddish-brown.

Range and Habitat A recently described species known only from central-eastern Rhodesia (Umtali).

CHARAXES ETHALION Boisduval
Satyr Charaxes

p 160

Identification Wingspan 5–6½cm. Broad forewing with outer margin straight; ♂ black without bluish or greenish sheen; single pale spot in forewing cell, sometimes absent; hindwing with reddish or green marginal markings; two tails: underside uniform reddish-brown. ♀ larger and extremely variable; median band may be blue or white, sometimes ochreous; forewing band straight or curved: paler reddish-brown on underside.

Range and Habitat Forests, woodland and thick bush country in Kenya, eastern Uganda, south through Tanzania to Zambia, Malawi, Mozambique and Rhodesia to South Africa. In the south flies from September to April; throughout the year further north.

Larval Food Plants *Albizia*.

CHARAXES ETHEOCLES Cramer
Black Forest Charaxes

p 160

Identification Wingspan 5–6cm. ♂ dark bluish-black with or without greenish-blue spots near the costa of forewing; with or without white submarginal spots on hindwing; two tails; underside may be grey with distinct black markings or brown with markings indistinct. ♀ variable: blackish-brown with bluish-white median band and white or ochreous spots; or blackish with more or less heavy blue spots in place of median band.

Range and Habitat Forest areas throughout tropical Africa from West Africa to western Kenya and western Tanzania. Flies throughout the year.

Larval Food Plants *Scutia*.

CHARAXES BAILEYI van Someren
Bailey's Charaxes

Identification Wingspan 5½–
6cm. ♂ blue-black with
strong blue sheen towards
base; one, two, or three small
bluish spots along forewing
costa; greyish marginal
markings; bluish-white submarginal spots on hindwing
and admarginal greenish line
present; underside deep grey
with dark markings. ♀ deep
blue-black with blue sheen
at base; bluish spots on forewing and broad blue band on
hindwing; sometimes blue
hindwing band relatively narrow.

Range and Habitat A recently described species with a very restricted distribution in western highlands of Kenya – eastern Mau Forest, Molo, Visoi
Gap, Eldama Ravine and Sabukia. Inhabits forested areas and riverine
wooded areas. Flies throughout the year.
Larval Food Plants *Scutia.*

CHARAXES CEDREATUS Hewitson   p 160

Identification Wingspan 5½–
6½cm. ♂ blue-black with bluish-green basal sheen; row of
white elongated submarginal
spots on hindwing: two tails:
underside silvery-grey with
dark markings. ♀ has apical
area black with white spots
and a curved white band;
basal half olive-brown; hindwing olive-brown, black
marginal border with bluish-

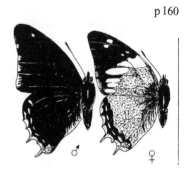

white spots: a second form of ♀ has blue patches on fore and hindwings.
Range and Habitat Forests of West Africa and the Congo, eastwards to
Uganda, western Tanzania and western Kenya. Flies throughout the year.
Larval Food Plants *Scutia.*

CHARAXES VIRILIS Rothschild   p 160
Identification Wingspan $5\frac{1}{2}$–$6\frac{1}{2}$cm. ♂ blue-black with a brilliant blue sheen; one or two blue spots below costa; strongly marked white submarginal spots on hind-wing: two tails: underside purplish red-brown with dark markings indistinct. ♀ resembles ♂ but larger with longer tails; sometimes a few blue spots on forewing. Best distinguished from related species by brilliant blue sheen on upperside of wings.
Range and Habitat An uncommon and local species found in forests in West Africa, the Congo and Uganda. Flies throughout the year.
Larval Food Plants *Adenanthera pavonina*.

♀

CHARAXES CATACHROUS Staudinger
Identification Wingspan $5\frac{1}{2}$–$6\frac{1}{2}$cm. ♂ black with some bluish sheen; with or without small blue spots below forewing costa; small white submarginal spots on hind-wing; underside mainly silvery-white. ♀ blackish-brown with creamy or pale ochreous markings on forewing, and a narrow white median band and sub-marginal white spots on hindwing; under-side mainly silvery as in ♂. Best disting-uished from *Charaxes etheocles* by its silvery underside. One form of ♀ in east-ern race has a curved white median band on forewing.
Range and Habitat Forests of West Africa, the Congo, Uganda and western Kenya, with an eastern race – *Charaxes catachrous contraria* (which may be specifically distinct from nominate *catachrous*) – in the coastal forests of Kenya and in eastern Tanzania. Flies throughout the year.
Larval Food Plants *Scutia myrtina*.

♀

CHARAXES BERKELEYI van Someren & Jackson

Identification Wingspan 5½–6½cm. ♂ bluish-black with two small white apical spots and two or three bluish spots below costa of forewing; wavy greenish line and submarginal bluish-white spots on hindwing; two tails: underside dark greyish with silvery sheen; hindwings tend to reddish. ♀ black with bluish sheen: markings on forewing ochreous to orange-brown; hindwing median band white, margined with blue; submarginal blue spots; tails longer than in ♂; underside silvery-grey with whitish median bands.

Range and Habitat High level forest, Kenya, mainly east of the Rift Valley.

Larval Food Plants *Scutia.*

CHARAXES AUBYNI van Someren & Jackson

Identification Wingspan 5½–6½cm. ♂ black with a greenish sheen; two apical whitish spots and two pale spots below forewing costa; wavy green post-discal line on hindwing and line of small bluish-white submarginal spots; two tails. Similar to ♂ *Charaxes viola* but larger. Underside dark brownish-grey with satiny bars. ♀ brownish-black with slight greenish sheen; creamy-white spots and median bands; underside as in ♂.

Range and Habitat Wooded and forested areas in Kenya (Teita Hills and highlands east of Rift Valley), highlands of northern and southern Tanzania and Malawi. Flies throughout the year.

Larval Food Plants *Albizia gummifera* and *Albizia sassa.*

CHARAXES VIOLA Butler p 160

Viola Charaxes

Identification Wingspan 5½–6½cm. ♂ bluish-black, forewing margin with greyish-green spots; two apical bluish-white spots and two or three spots below costa; submarginal band of spots present in some examples; hindwing with submarginal bluish-white spots; greenish-blue wavy line sometimes present: two tails: underside pale greyish-brown, sometimes slightly reddish with black markings. In Kenya and southern races ♂ less heavily marked. ♀ blackish-brown with orange-brown marginal spots; forewing median band orange to whitish; hindwing band bluish-white; submarginal blue spots; tails longer than in ♂. In the southern race, *Charaxes viola phaeus*, the ♂ has very restricted spotting; the ♀ has the apical half of forewing black with white spots, the basal half bright blue to greyish-blue; some specimens possess a curved white median band; hindwing bright blue to greyish-blue with blue spots on black marginal band. Underside grey to pale reddish-brown. The closely related *Charaxes manica* has a deep red-brown to purplish-red underside with indistinct markings.

Range and Habitat A woodland, savannah and bush country species found in most parts of the Ethiopian Region in suitable habitats: the southern race occurs mainly in Brachystegia woodland from central Tanzania to South Africa. Flies throughout the year.

Larval Food Plants *Acacia mellifera*, *Acacia caffra*, *Albizia sassa*, *Entada* and *Albizia gummifera*.

CHARAXES MANICA Trimen

Identification Wingspan 5½–7½cm. ♂ blue-black with two whitish apical spots and two bluish spots below forewing costa; hindwing with little trace of submarginal spots; wavy green post-discal line sometimes present; underside dark purplish red-brown. ♀ very similar to two principal ♀ forms of *Charaxes viola phaeus* with extensive blue or greenish-blue basal

areas; with or without white median band on forewing; distinguished by larger size and dark reddish underside.

Range and Habitat Woodlands and bush country in Tanzania, Malawi, Mozambique, Zambia, the southern Congo and Rhodesia.

Larval Food Plants *Albizia*.

CHARAXES FULGURATA Aurivillius

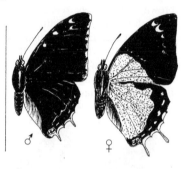

Identification Wingspan 5½–7 cm. ♂ black with greenish sheen at base; crescent-shaped greenish-blue markings in apical and costal area of forewing; row of bluish-white submarginal spots on hindwing; two tails. ♀ variable, basal half of wings blue or greenish-blue; with or without white median band on forewing; large crescent-shaped apical spots; tails longer than in ♂.

Range and Habitat A local and uncommon species found in northern Angola, southern Congo (Katanga), north-western Rhodesia. Occurs mainly in Brachystegia woodland and bush country.

Larval Food Plants *Acacia*.

CHARAXES USAMBARAE van Someren & Jackson

Identification Wingspan 6½–8½cm. ♂ a large black charaxes with deeply serrated margins of fore and hindwings and two long tails; two small blue apical spots and one or two spots below costa of forewing; a few bluish submarginal spots on hindwing. Its large size, deeply serrated wing margins and long tails distinguish this species from all mainland *Charaxes*, although *Char-*

axes pembanus, a species found only on Pemba Island off the Tanzanian coast, is closely related but has a less concave forewing margin. ♀ blackish-brown, paler towards base; curved white forewing band and white spots; hindwing with broad white band with strong violet-blue suffusion at edges. ♀ *Charaxes pembanus* has two bands of creamy-white spots on forewing, and a creamy-white band on hindwing.

Range and Habitat A rare species known only from the forests of the Usambara Mts. in north-eastern Tanzania.

CHARAXES NICHETES Grose-Smith

p 113

Water Charaxes
Identification Wingspan 6–7½cm. ♂ margin of forewing deeply concave; orange to deep reddish-brown with dark brown or blackish markings; submarginal ocelli on hindwing; no tails. ♀ larger and paler. West African race darker and more richly coloured than race found in Mozambique and Rhodesia.

Range and Habitat An uncommon and local forest charaxes found in West Africa and the Congo to Uganda (Entebbe) and in Zambia, Malawi, Mozambique and Rhodesia. Inhabits forested areas, thick bush and woodland, especially along rivers and streams. Flies throughout the year.

Larval Food Plants *Uapaca*.

CHARAXES PORTHOS Grose-Smith

p 160

Identification Wingspan 7–8cm. ♂ margin of forewing deeply concave; blue-black with a blue spot just before forewing cell; bright blue band across wings; row of submarginal bluish spots on hindwing; no tails. ♀ resembles ♂ but larger and blue band tinted violet; one short tail on hindwing.

Range and Habitat An uncommon forest species found in West Africa and the Congo, east to Uganda. Flies throughout the year.

NYMPHALIDAE – CHARAXES

1 **CHARAXES ETHALION** ♂ ♀ ♀ ♀   *page* 153
♂ black with few or no markings: underside dark reddish-brown:
♀♀ very variable: underside reddish.

2 **CHARAXES VIRILIS** ♂   155
Sexes similar: bright blue sheen on wings.

3 **CHARAXES VIOLA PICTA** ♂ ♀   156
Underside brownish-grey.

4 **CHARAXES VIOLA PHAEUS** ♂ ♀ ♀   157
Underside brownish-grey.

5 **CHARAXES GUDERIANA** ♂ ♀   151
♂ large white spots on forewing: ♀ like small edition of *Charaxes
achaemenes* ♀ but underside quite different: see text.

6 **CHARAXES CEDREATUS** ♂ ♀ ♀   154
♂ row of narrow, elongated white submarginal streaks on hindwing:
♀ like miniature ♀ of *Charaxes tiridates* or ♀ *Charaxes smaragdalis*.

7 **CHARAXES ETHEOCLES** ♂ ♀   153
♂ with or without round white marginal spots on hindwing: ♀ may be
blue-spotted, or white-spotted on forewing with white hindwing
band.

8 **CHARAXES ZELICA** ♂   162
♂ blue spots across forewing: ♀ like ♂ but with short tail on
hindwing.

9 **CHARAXES LAODICE** ♂ ♀   162
♂ large blue submarginal spots on fore and hindwings: ♀ tailed.

10 **CHARAXES DOUBLEDAYI** ♂   163
♂ slightly rounded spots on margin of hindwing: see text: ♀ larger
with short tail on hindwing.

11 **CHARAXES PORTHOS** ♂   159
♂ round white submarginal spots on hindwing: ♀ larger with tail on
hindwing.

1

2

3 ♂

3 ♀

4 ♂

4 ♀

5 ♂

5 ♀

6

7 ♂

7 ♀

8

9

10

11

12

13

PLATE 18   161

NYMPHALIDAE

1 **PALLA USSHERI** ♂   *page* 164
  ♂ white band restricted mainly to forewing: ♀ brown with wide white
  band.

2 **PALLA DECIUS** ♂   164
  ♂ white band extends half way across hindwing: ♀ brown with
  relatively narrow white band: see text.

3 **CYMOTHOE BECKERI** ♂ ♀   166
  ♂ brown marginal band: ♀ orange patch on hindwing.

4 **CYMOTHOE LURIDA** ♂ ♀   166
  ♂ narrow brown marginal band: ♀ broad white band across wings.

5 **CYMOTHOE THEOBENE** ♂ ♀   165
  Brown basal patch.

6 **CYMOTHOE EGESTA** ♂   166
  ♂ blackish markings on fore and hindwings: ♀ with narrow white
  band across wings.

7 **CYMOTHOE SANGARIS** ♂ ♀   167
  ♂ bright blood-red: ♀ with or without red at base of wings.

8 **BYBLIA ILITHYIA** ♂   175
  Sexes similar: row of black spots on hindwing.

9 **BYBLIA ACHELOIA** ♂   178
  Sexes similar: no row of black spots on hindwing.

10 **EUPHAEDRA NEOPHRON** ♂   168
  Sexes similar: violet with orange band on forewing.

11 **EUPHAEDRA RUSPINA** ♂   169
  Sexes similar: angular projection on hindwing.

12 **EUPHAEDRA ELEUS** ♂   169
  Sexes similar: variable in colour, from dark red-brown to greenish
  brown.

13 **EUPHAEDRA SPATIOSA** ♂   168
  Sexes similar: dark olive-brown with yellow forewing bar.

CHARAXES ZELICA Butler   p 160

Identification Wingspan 7–8cm. ♂ blue-black with subapical blue spot and row of blue spots across forewing; band of blue spots on hindwing and submarginal row of small bluish-white dots: no tails. ♀ larger and blue markings tinged violet; single short tail on hindwing.

Range and Habitat Forest areas of West Africa and the Congo, east to Uganda, western Tanzania and western Kenya. Flies throughout the year.

CHARAXES LAODICE Drury   p 160

Identification Wingspan 6–7½cm. ♂ margin of forewing deeply concave; blue-black with row of large bright blue submarginal spots on fore and hindwings; two blue spots in front of forewing cell; no tails. ♀ larger with reddish-brown marginal band on fore and hindwings and a single tail on hindwing.

Range and Habitat Forests of West Africa and the Congo to western Uganda and western Tanzania. Flies throughout the year.

CHARAXES MYCERINA Godart

Identification Wingspan 6½–8½cm. ♂ margin of forewing deeply concave; blue-black with a blue basal patch in cell of forewing; blue spots below costa and a band of large submarginal blue spots; blue band across hindwing and band of narrow elongated blue spots along margin of hindwing; no tails. ♂ *Charaxes doubledayi* is very similar but marginal blue spots on hindwing are larger and more rounded and do not form a continuous line as they do in *Charaxes mycerina*. ♀ resembles ♂ but larger; blue markings with violet tinge;

single tail on hindwing. Like the ♂ it differs from *Charaxes doubledayi* in having narrow elongated blue marginal spots on hindwing.

Range and Habitat An uncommon forest species found in West Africa and the Congo.

CHARAXES DOUBLEDAYI Aurivillius   p 160

Identification Wingspan 7–8cm. ♂ margin of forewing deeply concave; blue-black with basal blue patch in forewing cell and blue spots below costa; large blue submarginal spots on forewing and blue band across hindwing; large rounded blue spots on margin of hindwing, not forming an almost continuous line as in *Charaxes mycerina*; no tails. ♀ larger, with violet-blue markings and short tail on hindwing; marginal spots rounded, not narrow and elongated as in ♀ *Charaxes mycerina*.

Range and Habitat Forests of West Africa and the Congo; local and uncommon. Flies throughout the year.

PALLA PUBLIUS Staudinger
Identification Wingspan 7–8cm.
♂ forewing blackish-brown
with broad white band; hindwing blackish-brown with
broad white band merging to
orange towards hind margin;
single tail. ♀ resembles ♂ but
ill-defined yellowish-white submarginal spots on forewing.
Range and Habitat Forest
species found in West Africa
and the Congo. Also recorded
from Mukuyu in western Tanzania. Flies throughout the year.

PALLA USSHERI Butler   p 161
Identification Wingspan 6½–8
cm. ♂ blackish-brown with a
white band across forewing;
hindwing with broad orange
band, white restricted to costal
margin; one tail. ♀ orange-
brown with dark brown markings and a whitish median band
across both wings. This is a
much paler butterfly than ♀♀ of
related species.
Range and Habitat Forests of
West Africa, the Congo, Uganda and western Tanzania. Flies
throughout the year.
Larval Food Plants *Porana densi-
flora, Toddalia aculeata.*

PALLA DECIUS Cramer   p 161
Identification Wingspan 7–8cm. ♂ forewing blackish-brown with a white
median band tinged on inner side with pale blue; hindwing with white band

merging to orange towards hind angle; tailed. The similar ♂ *Palla violinitens* has white band tinged with violet-blue on both inner and outer sides. ♀ dark brown with white spots and a white band which becomes narrow at forewing costa, distinguishing this species from ♀ *Palla violinitens* in which the white band is wide at the costa.

Range and Habitat Forests of West Africa and the Congo. Flies throughout the year.

PALLA VIOLINITENS Crowley

Identification Wingspan 7–8cm. ♂ blackish-brown with a white median band across both wings tinged strongly violet-blue on both inner and outer sides; orange restricted to small patch near anal angle of hindwing; tailed. The similar ♂ *Palla decius* has more orange on hindwing and white median band tinged blue on inner side only. ♀ dark brown with whitish markings and white band which is wide at costa of forewing, not narrow as in ♀ *Palla decius*.

Range and Habitat Forest areas of West Africa and the Congo.

CYMOTHOE THEOBENE Doubleday   p 161

Identification Wingspan 5½–7cm. ♂ rich dark brown with a buff or golden-yellow median band and yellow spotting or mottling in the wide dark brown marginal band; ♀ larger, whitish with dark brown markings; in some examples, the white is replaced by brown.

Range and Habitat Forests and heavily wooded areas of West Africa and the Congo eastwards to Kenya and Tanzania, south to Malawi. Flies throughout the year.

Larval Food Plants *Rinorea, Dorvyalis.*

CYMOTHOE BECKERI Schaffer   p 161

Identification Wingspan 6½–8½cm. ♂ margins of wings scalloped; orange-buff with broad yellow median patches on fore and hindwings; orange-spotted dark brown border. ♀ quite different, black with white spots, a whitish basal patch and an orange patch on hindwing.

Range and Habitat Forests of West Africa and the Congo to Uganda. Flies throughout the year.

CYMOTHOE EGESTA Cramer   p 161

Identification Wingspan 7–9cm. ♂ ochreous-orange with dark markings on fore and hindwings; hindwing much darker than in related ♂ *Cymothoe lurida.* ♀ greyish-brown with narrow whitish band across wings and whitish subapical patch on forewing; ♀ *Cymothoe lurida* has a broader band on forewing.

Range and Habitat A forest species found in West Africa, the Congo, western Tanzania and Uganda. Flies throughout the year.

CYMOTHOE LURIDA Butler   p 161

Identification Wingspan 7–9cm. ♂ bright ochreous-orange with narrow dark brown apex and narrow dark marginal band on fore and hindwings; dark

submarginal line and spots on
hindwing. ♀ brownish-grey with
irregular broad whitish band on
forewing and dark markings.
Range and Habitat Forest areas of
West Africa and the Congo, east to
Uganda and western Kenya. Flies
throughout the year.

CYMOTHOE SANGARIS Godart   p 161
Blood Red Cymothoe
Identification Wingspan 6–7cm. ♂ brilliant blood-red with a very small blackish-
brown apex and small blackish submarginal spots on hindwing: sometimes indistinct black submarginal dots present
on forewing. ♀ pale greyish-brown with
dark markings, to orange-brown at base
of wings. In addition to *Cymothoe sangaris*
there are several other species in which
the ♂♂ are red: *C. coccinata*, bright pale
orange-red with well-defined submarginal dots on fore and hindwings; *C. anitorgis*

which is bright scarlet-red with a large white spot on the costa of the hindwing; and *C. ogova* which is dark orange-red with some crescent-shaped
marginal spots on the hindwing. All are West African/Congo species.
Range and Habitat Forests of West Africa and the Congo to Uganda, western
Tanzania and western Kenya. Flies throughout the year.

CRENIDOMIMAS CONCORDIA Hopffer
Speckled Lilac Nymph
Identification Wingspan 4½–5cm. ♂ violet or
lilac-blue with heavy marginal and forewing
markings; underside orange-brown with submarginal black-dotted blue spots and central
blue patch with black streaks on hindwing.
Sexes alike. In the very similar *Asterope rosa* the
♂ is violet with a row of small submarginal dark
spots on forewing; underside deep orange, the
hindwing crossed by pale blue bands and a blue
submarginal line.

Range and Habitat Woodland areas from Tanzania to Mozambique, Malawi, Zambia, Rhodesia and Angola. Local but sometimes not uncommon. Flies around bushes and small trees. On the wing throughout the year.

EUPHAEDRA NEOPHRON Hopffer   p 161
Gold Banded Forester

Identification Wingspan 6–7½cm. ♂ apical half of forewing black crossed by wide orange band; tip of apex orange; basal half of forewing and hindwing bluish-violet with or without a dark marginal band. Sexes alike, but ♀ larger. Underside drab greyish-brown.

Range and Habitat Coastal forests, woodlands and plantations from eastern Kenya south through Tanzania to Mozambique, Malawi and eastern Rhodesia to Natal, South Africa. Flies rapidly very near the ground amongst thick cover, but settles on the ground frequently, with wings flat. On the wing throughout the year.
Larval Food Plants *Deinbollia.*

EUPHAEDRA SPATIOSA Mabille   p 161

Identification Wingspan 8½–11½cm. ♂ fore and hindwings dark olive-brown with a white tip on apex of forewing and a narrow orange-yellow subapical band. Sexes similar but ♀ usually larger.

Range and Habitat A forest species from West Africa and the Congo to Uganda and western Tanzania. Flies close to the ground, resting with wings flat: much attracted to fermenting fruit.
Larval Food Plants *Phialodiscus, Paulinnia.*

EUPHAEDRA ELEUS Drury
Orange Forester
p 161

Identification Wingspan 7½–10½cm. Variable in colour from dark red-brown or orange-brown to greenish-brown; apical half of forewing black with subapical white bar; hindwing scalloped, broad black margin with round white spots; anal angle of hindwing rounded, not sharply angled. Sexes alike, but ♀ usually larger. The similar *Euphaedra ruspina* is smaller, brighter orange and has sharply angled anal angle on hindwing.

Range and Habitat Forests of West Africa and the Congo to Uganda, western Tanzania and western Kenya. Flies throughout the year.

EUPHAEDRA RUSPINA Hewitson
p 161

Identification Wingspan 7½–10cm. ♂ bright orange-brown with black apical patch crossed by short white bar; hindwing with black marginal band spotted with white; anal angle of hindwing sharply angled. ♀ like ♂ but usually larger and paler. *Euphaedra eleus* has rounded hindwing.

Range and Habitat West Africa and the Congo to Uganda. Inhabits forests, flies near the ground, often in shade. Can be attracted by decaying fruit such as bananas and pineapples.

HAMANUMIDA DAEDALUS Fabricius
Guineafowl
p 176

Identification Wingspan 5–6cm. Uniformly leaden grey with rows of black-edged white dots; small white patch on apex of forewing; underside orange-brown. Sexes alike but ♀ usually larger.

Range and Habitat A common species throughout the Ethiopian Region in bush and savannah country. Flies close to the ground; often settles on bare earth with wings spread flat. Flies throughout the year.

Larval Food Plants *Combretum*.

ATERICA GALENE Brown p 176
Forest Glade Nymph
Identification Wingspan 5½–8cm. ♂
blackish-brown with two bands of
creamy-yellow spots on forewing and
a creamy-yellow patch on hindwing;
♀ larger with white or creamy-yellow
spots on forewing; hindwing patch
larger than in ♂ and variable in colour,
white, creamy-yellow or orange-
brown.
Range and Habitat A common species
found in forests throughout tropical
Africa south to Mozambique, Malawi
and eastern Rhodesia. Flies close to
the ground in forest shade. On the
wing throughout the year.
Larval Food Plants *Quisqualis*.

CYNANDRA OPIS Drury p 176
Blue Banded Nymph
Identification Wingspan 4½–5½cm. ♂
blackish with brilliant blue iridescent
bars. ♀ larger, dark brown with
creamy-yellow markings.
Range and Habitat Forest areas of
West Africa and the Congo east to
Uganda. Flies close to the ground
amongst forest undergrowth; blue
iridescence of ♂ very striking in field.
Flies throughout the year.

PSEUDARGYNNIS HEGEMONE Godart p 176
False Fritillary
Identification Wingspan 5–5½cm.
Orange-brown with numerous black
dots and spots, and heavier markings
along forewing costa; underside with
oblique reddish stripe. Sexes alike.
The similar *Phalanta phalantha* has
different wing shape and markings.

Range and Habitat Inhabits swampy grasslands and bush in West Africa south to Zambesi River. Flies throughout the year.

PSEUDONEPTIS COENOBITA Fabricius

p 176

Identification Wingspan 5–6cm. ♂ blackish-brown with pale blue bands and markings. ♀ slightly larger and paler.
Range and Habitat Forests of West Africa and the Congo, east to Uganda and western Kenya. Flies in forest shade, sometimes close to the ground. On the wing throughout the year.

CATUNA CRITHEA Drury

Identification Wingspan 6–7cm. Pale greyish-brown with dark brown and pale yellow markings; a broad creamy-yellow longitudinal band across hindwing. Sexes similar, but ♀ usually larger.
Range and Habitat A common forest species ranging from West Africa and the Congo east to Uganda, western Tanzania and western Kenya. Flies close to the ground in forest shade; attracted to fermenting fruits. Flies throughout the year.

PSEUDACRAEA SEMIRE Cramer

p 176

Identification Wingspan 6–7cm. ♂ blackish-brown with bright pale green spots on forewing and pale green basal patch on hindwing; band of red-brown spots on hindwing. Sexes similar but ♀ larger and paler.
Range and Habitat A West African forest species which ranges eastwards through the Congo to western Uganda, where it has been recorded in the Bwamba and Budongo Forests.

PSEUDACRAEA BOISDUVALI Doubleday   p 176
Trimen's False Acraea

Identification Wingspan 9–10cm. Many of the pseudacraeas mimic members of the genera *Bematistes* and *Acraea* (Acraeidae), but may be distinguished by the open hindwing cell: in the acraeas the cell is closed. *Pseudacraea boisduvali* is bright red with black spots and a red-spotted black marginal band on hindwing: the East and South African race, *P. b. trimeni*, has a broad orange bar in the apical half of forewing, whilst in the nominate race the apical area is darker. Sexes similar but ♀ larger.

Range and Habitat Forests and wooded country throughout tropical Africa south to Natal, South Africa. Flies throughout the year.

Larval Food Plants *Chrysophyllum, Mimusops.*

PSEUDACRAEA EURYTUS Linnaeus   p 176
False Wanderer

Identification Wingspan 7–8cm. Very variable species mimicking various species of *Bematistes*. ♂ blackish-brown with forewing band white, orange, or orange-brown; very broad white or orange-brown band on hindwing. ♀ usually with white bands on fore and hindwings.

Range and Habitat A forest and woodland species ranging from West to East Africa, southwards to Natal and eastern Cape Province, South Africa. Flies throughout the year.

Larval Food Plants *Chrysophyllum.*

PSEUDACRAEA POGGEI Dewitz   p 176
Identification Wingspan 7–8½cm. Margins of fore and hindwings scalloped; bright orange-brown, with or without a black apical patch; white subapical

bar and white marginal spots on forewing; veins blackened; narrow black
marginal band. Sexes alike. Mimics
Danaus chrysippus.
Range and Habitat Inhabits Brachystegia woodlands in Tanzania, Malawi,
Zambia, Rhodesia, southern Congo
(Katanga) and Angola: uncommon
and local. This insect has a buoyant,
sailing flight very similar to that of its model.

PSEUDACRAEA LUCRETIA Cramer p 176
False Diadem
Identification Wingspan 7–8cm. Variable; blackish-brown with broad white
or ochreous median band on forewing, two or more white subapical
spots and a white tip to the apex; hindwing with white or ochreous patch or
band. Sexes alike.
Range and Habitat A common species
in forests and wooded areas through-
out the Ethiopian Region. Flies throughout the year.
Larval Food Plants *Chrysophyllum, Mimusops.*

NEPTIS SACLAVA Boisduval p 176
Small Spotted Sailer
Identification Wingspan 4–4½cm. The genus
Neptis contains over 40 species of small or
medium-sized black and white butterflies,
many of which are difficult to identify. They
have a characteristic sailing flight amongst
trees and bushes. *Neptis saclava* has the
forewing subapical white spots smaller than
the central spot; on the underside there is a
row of brown spots on the hindwing before
the marginal rows of white lines. Sexes alike.
Range and Habitat A common species
throughout the Ethiopian Region in wood-
land, forest margins, bush and savannah country. Flies throughout the year.
Larval Food Plants *Acalypha, Combretum.*

CYRESTIS CAMILLUS Fabricius   p 176
African Map Butterfly

Identification Wingspan 5–5½cm. Delicate white species with well-developed tail on hindwing; narrow brown marginal bands and orange and brown bands across wings. Sexes similar.

Range and Habitat Forest and wooded areas in West Africa and the Congo, east to Uganda and Kenya, south to Mozambique, Malawi and eastern Rhodesia. Attracted to damp mud or sand on stream banks; settles with wings spread flat. Flies throughout the year.

ASTEROPE ROSA Hewitson   p 176
Lilac Nymph

Identification Wingspan 4½–5cm. ♂ violet-blue; line of small dark submarginal spots on fore and hindwings; underside deep orange with black-streaked pale blue bands across hindwing. ♀ similar, but with heavier dark markings. Resembles *Crenidomimas concordia*, but this species has scattered dark markings on upperside; underside with central blue patch, not blue bands.

Range and Habitat Occurs in savannah, bush and wooded areas of southern Tanzania, Mozambique, Malawi, Zambia, eastern Rhodesia and northern Natal, South Africa. Flies throughout the year.

ASTEROPE OCCIDENTALIUM Mabille
Velvety Nymph

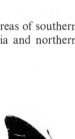

Identification Wingspan 5–5½cm. Deep velvety black-brown with slight purplish sheen; hindwing paler towards margin with eyespots; underside, forewing orange-brown with dark brown apical band; hindwing greyish with dark brown markings. Sexes similar.

Range and Habitat A common forest species, often appearing in swarms on forest roads, in West Africa, the Congo east to Uganda, western Tanzania, Kenya and Ethiopia. Flies throughout the year.

ASTEROPE MORANTI Trimen
Obscure Tree Nymph

Identification Wingspan 5–5½cm. ♂ dull brown, darker on apex and margins; underside greyish with ill-defined dark markings. ♀ with dark patch on forewing and whitish spots below costa.

Range and Habitat Forests and wooded areas in eastern Kenya, Tanzania, to Malawi, Mozambique, eastern Rhodesia and South Africa. Flies throughout the year.

♂

ASTEROPE BOISDUVALI Wallengren
Brown Tree Nymph

Identification Wingspan 5–5½cm. ♂ warm pale brown with blackish markings on forewing; hindwing with marginal black line and small submarginal black spots. Sexes similar, but ♀ with heavier dark markings.

Range and Habitat A common species, often in swarms, of forested and wooded country over most of the Ethiopian Region. Flies throughout the year.

Larval Food Plants *Excoecaria*.

♀

BYBLIA ILITHYIA Drury p 161
Joker

Identification Wingspan 5–5½cm. Bright orange with irregular black bands and markings across the wings. Sexes similar. This species may be distinguished from the similar *Byblia acheloia* by the presence of a median row of black spots on the hindwing.

♂

NYMPHALIDAE – NYMPHALIDS

1 **HAMANUMIDA DAEDALUS** ♂   *page* 169
   Sexes similar: grey speckled with white.
2 **ATERICA GALENE** ♂ ♀ ♀   170
   Hindwing patch in ♀ variable in size and colour.
3 **PSEUDONEPTIS COENOBITA** ♂   171
   Sexes similar: black with greenish-blue bands.
4 **CYNANDRA OPIS** ♂ ♀   170
   ♂ black with dark blue iridescence.
5 **PSEUDARGYNNIS HEGEMONE** ♂   170
   Sexes similar: compare with *Phalanta phalantha* (16).
6 **CYRESTIS CAMILLUS** ♂   174
   Sexes similar: white with narrow orange and dark brown bands.
7 **PSEUDACRAEA SEMIRE** ♂   171
   Sexes similar: pale green spots.
8 **PSEUDACRAEA BOISDUVALI BOISDUVALI** ♂   172
   Sexes similar: forewing mainly greyish.
9 **PSEUDACRAEA BOISDUVALI TRIMENI** ♂   172
   Sexes similar: forewing basal half red.
10 **PSEUDACRAEA EURYTUS** ♂ ♀   172
   Species extremely variable, mimicking species of *Bematistes* (Acraeidae).
11 **PSEUDACRAEA LUCRETIA** ♂ ♀   173
   Dark brown with white and/or creamy markings.
12 **PSEUDACRAEA POGGEI** ♂ ♂   172
   Sexes similar: serrated hindwing margin: mimics *Danaus chrysippus*
   (Danaidae).
13 **ASTEROPE ROSA** ♂   174
   ♂ blue with dark spots close to outer margin, not scattered over wings
   as in *Crenidomimas concordia*: see text: ♀ with dark blotches on
   forewing.
14 **LACHNOPTERA AYRESII** ♂ ♀   197
   Silvery-grey scent patch on hindwing of ♂.
15 **PHALANTA COLUMBINA** ♂   197
   Sexes similar: hindwing angled.
16 **PHALANTA PHALANTHA** ♂   198
   Sexes similar: hindwing rounded: compare with *Pseudargynnis*
   hegemone (5).

1

2 ♂   2 ♀   2 ♀   3

4 ♂   4 ♀   5   6   7

8   9   10 ♂   10 ♀

11 ♂   11 ♀   12 ♂   12 ♂

13   14 ♂   14 ♀   15   16

PLATE 20   177

NYMPHALIDAE – NYMPHALIDS

1 **KALLIMA RUMIA** ♂ ♀   *page* 179
   ♂ violet-blue forewing band: ♀ broken white band on forewing.

2 **KALLIMA ANSORGEI** ♂   180
   Sexes similar: green basal area.

3 **KALLIMA CYMODOCE** ♂   180
   Sexes similar: blue basal area.

4 **KALLIMA JACKSONI** ♂   179
   Sexes similar: brilliant blue with reddish margin to hindwing.

5 **APATUROPSIS CLEOCHARIS** ♂ ♀   179
   Two white spots in apex of forewing.

6 **CATACROPTERA CLOANTHE** ♂   188
   Sexes similar: edge of hindwing tufted with short hairs.

7 **EURYTELA DRYOPE** ♂   178
   Sexes similar: orange-brown submarginal band.

8 **EURYTELA HIARBAS** ♂   178
   Sexes similar: white submarginal band.

9 **SALAMIS TEMORA** ♂ ♀   185
   Bright blue or violet-blue wings.

10 **SALAMIS CYTORA** ♂   186
   Sexes similar: blue or bluish-white band across wings.

11 **SALAMIS PARHASSUS** ♂   186
   Sexes similar: bright mother-of-pearl sheen.

12 **SALAMIS ANACARDII** ♂ ♂   187
   Sexes similar: slight mother-of-pearl sheen: extensive black markings
   on forewing.

13 **SALAMIS CACTA CACTA** ♂   187
   Sexes similar: orange forewing patch.

14 **SALAMIS CACTA AMANIENSIS** ♂   187
   Sexes similar: no orange patch on forewing.

Range and Habitat A common species throughout most of the Ethiopian Region in woodlands, bush and open country. Flies throughout the year.

BYBLIA ACHELOIA Wallengren   p 161
Common Joker

Identification Wingspan 5–5½cm. Bright orange-red with heavy black markings; no median row of black spots on hindwing. Sexes similar.

Range and Habitat An abundant species throughout the Ethiopian Region, in open woodlands, bush and savannah country. Flies throughout the year, often alongside *Byblia ilithyia*.

♂

EURYTELA DRYOPE Cramer   p 177
Golden Piper

Identification Wingspan 5–5½cm. ♂ brown with a wide orange-yellow sub-marginal band; underside reddish-brown. Sexes similar, but ♀ usually larger and paler.

Range and Habitat Inhabits wooded areas, savannah and heavy bush throughout the Ethiopian Region. Species has a buoyant, rather slow flight. Flies throughout the year.

Larval Food Plants *Ricinus*, *Tragia*.

♂

EURYTELA HIARBAS Drury   p 177
Pied Piper

Identification Wingspan 5–6cm. ♂ black with a narrow white (rarely ochreous) submarginal band on fore and hindwings. Sexes alike but ♀ usually larger.

Range and Habitat Forests and wooded areas throughout tropical Africa to South Africa. Flies throughout the year.

Larval Food Plants *Dalechampia*, *Tragia*.

♂

APATUROPSIS CLEOCHARIS Hewitson p 177
Painted Empress

Identification Wingspan 4½–5½cm.
Forewing deeply concave; ♂ deep
orange-brown, broad black apical
patch with white spots; hindwing triangular with sharp anal angle; orange-
red with blackish-brown marginal
border. ♀ larger, paler, and hindwing
rounded, not angular.

Range and Habitat Forest areas of the
Congo, Uganda and western Kenya, south to eastern border of Rhodesia;
uncommon and local. Flies throughout the year.

KALLIMA RUMIA Doubleday p 177
African Leaf Butterfly

Identification Wingspan 6½–8cm.
Anal angle of hindwing attenuated.
♂ dark brown with a broad median
violet-blue band and a narrow
orange-red apical band on forewing; hindwing dark brown. ♀
larger, dark brown with broken
white and ochreous band on forewing and white apical spots; black-
ringed submarginal spots on hind-
wing. Underside dull browns and greys resembling a dead leaf.

Range and Habitat Forests of West Africa, the Congo and Uganda. Flies
throughout the year. Sometimes attracted to fermenting fruit.

KALLIMA JACKSONI Sharpe p 177
Jackson's Leaf Butterfly

Identification Wingspan 5½–6½cm.
One of the most beautiful of
African butterflies. Anal angle of
hindwing attenuated and slightly
incurved. ♂ brilliant deep blue
with marginal band of white spots
and subapical white spots on forewing; broad brick-red marginal
band on hindwing enclosing black

and bluish-white elongated spots. Sexes similar. Underside reddish dead-leaf pattern.

Range and Habitat A very uncommon and local species found in north-eastern Congo, Uganda (Serere and Tororo) and western Kenya (east of Tororo). Inhabits open bush and woodland savannah, being partial to hillsides with scattered bush and small trees. Flies throughout the year.

KALLIMA CYMODOCE Cramer   p 177
Western Leaf Butterfly
Identification Wingspan 5½–6½cm. Anal angle of hindwing attenuated and incurved. ♂ blackish-brown with basal third of wings brilliant blue or greenish-blue; narrow deep orange apical band on forewing and apical pale spot. Sexes similar but ♀ usually larger and apical band paler; underside dead-leaf pattern.
Range and Habitat Forests of West Africa, the Congo and western Uganda: also recorded from Mihumo in western Tanzania. Flies throughout the year.

KALLIMA ANSORGEI Rothschild   p 177
Ansorge's Leaf Butterfly
Identification Wingspan 5½–6½cm. Anal angle of hindwing attenuated. ♂ blackish with basal half of wings bright deep green; whitish spot in apex. Sexes similar but ♀ usually larger; underside dark brown dead-leaf pattern.
Range and Habitat Uncommon and local forest species in Congo, Uganda and western Kenya. Flies throughout the year.

HYPOLIMNAS MISIPPUS Linnaeus   p 192
Diadem
Identification Wingspan 6½–8cm.

Sexes dissimilar; the ♀ mimics
Danaus chrysippus. ♂ velvety-black
with a round white patch edged
with blue or violet in centre of
wings; white apical patch. ♀
orange-red with black apical patch
and black marginal bands; white
subapical band and white spots in
apex; or black apical patch and
white subapical band may be
absent. Some examples have whit-

ish patch on hindwing. Open hindwing cell distinguishes ♀ from *Danaus chrysippus.*

Range and Habitat One of the commonest and most widely distributed
African butterflies, found throughout the Ethiopian Region in open country,
bush, woodlands and gardens. Flies throughout the year.

Larval Food Plants *Asystasia*, *Portulaca*.

HYPOLIMNAS ANTEVORTA Distant   p 192

Blue Banded Diadem

Identification Wingspan 8½–10cm. ♂ black with blue and white forewing
bands, and a row of blue submarginal spots; hindwing with relatively narrow
blue median band and blue submarginal spots. Sexes similar but ♀ larger and
paler.

Range and Habitat An uncommon and local species found in low altitude
forest in eastern Tanzania.

HYPOLIMNAS SALMACIS Drury   p 192
Blue Diadem

Identification Wingspan 8–10cm. ♂ black with extensive blue or violet-blue and white markings; two or three white subapical spots on forewing; row of bluish-white submarginal spots on hindwing. ♀ larger with more extensive white markings. The similar *Hypolimnas monteironis* has a black apex without white spots.

Range and Habitat A common forest species ranging from West Africa and the Congo to Uganda and western Kenya.

HYPOLIMNAS MONTEIRONIS Druce   p 192
Black-tipped Diadem

Identification Wingspan 7–9cm. ♂ black with broad blue and white bands across wings; apical area of forewing black without white spots; pale blue

submarginal spots on hindwing. ♀ similar but larger and usually with more white in bands.

Range and Habitat An uncommon forest species found in eastern Nigeria and the Cameroons, West Africa.

HYPOLIMNAS MECHOWI Dewitz p 192
Mechow's Diadem

Identification Wingspan 7½–8½cm. ♂♀ forewing black with a large white median patch and a smaller white subapical patch; row of small white submarginal spots; large white patch on hindwing with outer margin dusky and ill-defined; row of small submarginal spots. Forewing pattern and dusky marginal hindwing patch distinguish this species from related species.

Range and Habitat A local and uncommon species recorded from the Congo forests.

HYPOLIMNAS DINARCHA Hewitson p 192

Identification Wingspan 9–10½cm. ♂♀ forewing black with variable white patches and spots; hindwing brown with ochreous basal patch of varying size; row of white submarginal spots.

Range and Habitat A West African forest species which extends eastwards through the Congo to Uganda and western Kenya. Flies throughout the year.

HYPOLIMNAS DECEPTOR Trimen   p 192
Deceptive Diadem

Identification Wingspan 7½–8½cm. ♂♀ black to blackish-brown with two large white semi-translucent patches on forewing, but no row of white submarginal spots: large white semi-translucent patch on hindwing. *Hypolimnas dubius* has white along inner (lower) margin of forewing; this area is black in *Hypolimnas deceptor*.

Range and Habitat Inhabits forested and wooded areas and coastal bush from Kenya south to Malawi, Mozambique and Natal, South Africa. Flies from October to May in South Africa, throughout the year elsewhere.

Larval Food Plants *Fleurya*.

HYPOLIMNAS DUBIUS Beauvois   p 192
Variable Diadem

Identification Wingspan 7½–8½ cm. ♂♀ variable; black with white (not semi-translucent) patches on forewing; white always on inner margin of forewing; hindwing white with black border, with or without white submarginal spots. *Hypolimnas deceptor* has semi-translucent white markings and inner margin of forewing black.

Range and Habitat A forest and woodland species common throughout the Ethiopian Region. Flies throughout the year except in South Africa where it is on the wing from October to April.

Larval Food Plants *Fleurya*.

HYPOLIMNAS USAMBARA Ward   p 192
Usambara Diadem

Identification Wingspan 8–11cm. ♂ black with a large bluish-tinged white patch on inner margin of forewing and a smaller white subapical patch; hindwing bluish-white with a black border and an orange-red patch in anal angle. ♀ similar but larger.

Range and Habitat Forested areas, woodland and lush coastal bush in eastern Kenya and eastern Tanzania. Flies throughout the year.

SALAMIS TEMORA Felder   p 177
Blue Salamis

Identification Wingspan 7½–8½cm. ♂ brilliant violet-blue with a greyish border to hindwing; submarginal dark lines and spots. ♀ larger, blue area more restricted and wider greyish borders.

Range and Habitat A fairly common forest species in West Africa and the Congo, east to Uganda, Ethiopia, western Kenya and western Tanzania. Rather slow, buoyant flight, often settles on foliage. Flies throughout the year.

SALAMIS CYTORA Doubleday   p 177
Blue-banded Salamis
Identification Wingspan 7–8cm. ♂ brownish-black with a bluish median band across fore and hindwings. ♀ larger and median bands usually paler.
Range and Habitat A local and uncommon forest species found in the forests of Upper Guinea, West Africa. Flies throughout the year.

SALAMIS PARHASSUS Drury   p 177
Mother of Pearl
Identification Wingspan 7½–9cm. ♂ brilliant translucent pale green, with pearly and violet iridescence in certain lights; black apex, margin and sub-

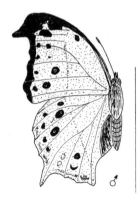

marginal spots on forewing; eyespots on hindwing; tailed. Sexes similar, but ♀ often larger.

Range and Habitat Forests and heavy woodland throughout the Ethiopian Region. Not a strong flier, alternately buoyant and jerky; often settles on foliage. Flies throughout the year.

Larval Food Plants *Asystasia, Isoglossa.*

SALAMIS ANACARDII Trimen

p 177

Clouded Mother of Pearl

Identification Wingspan 7–8½cm. ♂ white or creamy-white, sometimes with slight ochreous wash towards margins; heavy black markings; tailed. Far less mother-of-pearl sheen than in *Salamis parhassus*. Sexes similar but ♀ often larger.

Range and Habitat Savannah woodlands, coastal bush and forest margins throughout Ethiopian Region, south to Natal and Transvaal. Flies throughout the year except in south of its range when it is on the wing from October to April: at times gregarious.

p 177

SALAMIS CACTA Fabricius

Lilac Beauty

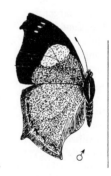

Identification Wingspan 6–7½cm. ♂ dark chestnut-brown with violet bloom; broad subapical orange band; apex and border blackish with three small white apical spots. Sexes similar but ♀ larger. The eastern race, *S. c. amaniensis*, has deeper violet bloom and usually lacks the orange subapical band; white apical spots larger and whiter.

Range and Habitat Forest areas of West Africa, the Congo, Uganda, Ethiopia, western Kenya and western Tanzania; the eastern race from eastern Tanzania to Mozambique and Malawi. Often flies in shady places in forest, and when settled sometimes difficult to disturb. Flies throughout the year.

CATACROPTERA CLOANTHE Cramer   p 177
Pirate

Identification Wingspan 5½–6cm. ♂
orange-brown with dark brown bars
and spots on forewing; row of submarginal blue-centred eyespots on
hindwing; margin of wings tufted with
tiny bristles; when newly emerged,
butterfly has a distinct pinkish-violet
bloom. Sexes alike but ♀ larger.

Range and Habitat Open country, bush
and savannah throughout the Ethiopian Region but not in large numbers.
Often found in swampy places. On the wing throughout the year except in
South Africa, where it flies from September to April.

Larval Food Plants *Justicia, Gomphocarpus.*

PRECIS TOUHILIMASA Vuillot   p 193
Naval Commander

Identification Wingspan 5½–6½cm. ♂
deep royal blue with a dark median
band across forewing and white apical
markings; reddish eyespots on fore
and hindwing. Sexes similar but ♀
usually larger.

Range and Habitat Brachystegia woodlands and bush, Zambia, southern
Congo and Angola: unconfirmed reports for Rhodesia. Reputed to be
common in the Zambian 'Copper Belt'.

PRECIS ARTAXIA Hewitson   p 193
Commodore

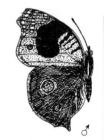

Identification Wingspan 5–6½cm. ♂
forewing dark royal blue with whitish
apical markings and a dark median
band; hindwing brown with two (one
large, one small) eyespots. Sexes
similar. Some seasonal difference in
size and shape.

Range and Habitat Inhabits Brachystegia woodland, bush and savannah country in Rhodesia, Zambia, Malawi, southern Tanzania and Mozambique, to southern Congo and Angola.

PRECIS NATALICA Felder   p 193
Brown Commodore

Identification Wingspan 5–6cm. ♂ deeply concave forewing; brown with dark brown and reddish-brown markings; white spots in apical area; hindwing with rounded reddish spots. Sexes similar but ♀ usually larger.

Range and Habitat Wooded and savannah country and open bush, eastern Kenya south through Tanzania, Mozambique, Malawi, Zambia, southern Congo, Angola, Rhodesia and South Africa. Flies throughout the year except in South Africa where it appears from October to April.
Larval Food Plants *Asystasia.*

PRECIS TEREA Drury   p 193
Soldier Commodore

Identification Wingspan 4½–5½cm. ♂ dark brown with a curved ochreous median band across both wings; row of submarginal eyespots on hindwing. ♀ similar but larger and ochreous band wider.

Range and Habitat Forested and wooded areas throughout the Ethiopian Region: often common in gardens. Flies throughout the year except in south of range where on the wing from October to April.
Larval Food Plants *Asystasia.*

PRECIS ARCHESIA Cramer   p 193
Garden Inspector

Identification Wingspan 5–6½cm. ♂ deep brown with a row of red-brown eyespots on fore and hindwings; two rows of bluish spots on apical area of fore-

wing; the wet season form is smaller
and forewing margin is less angled;
eyespots yellowish, not red. Sexes
similar but ♀ usually larger.
Range and Habitat Locally common
throughout most of the Ethiopian
Region in open bush country, savannah and in gardens. Flies throughout
the year.
Larval Food Plants *Coleus*, *Plectranthus*.

PRECIS TUGELA Trimen   p 193
Eared Commodore
Identification Wingspan 4½–6cm. ♂
brown with a broad orange-red band
across fore and hindwings; apex of
forewing very long and angled downwards in dry season form; underside
resembles dead leaf. Sexes similar.
Range and Habitat Forested and
wooded areas from the Congo,
Uganda and Kenya, south to Natal
and Transvaal, South Africa. Flies
throughout the year.

PRECIS CERYNE Boisduval   p 193
Marsh Commodore
Identification Wingspan 4½–5½cm. ♂
basal area brown; broad pale median
band across both wings yellowish towards base, orange-red towards margin; bluish submarginal band; dry
season form has more angular forewing margin. Sexes similar.
Range and Habitat Common in
swampy open country and bush near
water throughout the Ethiopian
Region south to Mozambique and
South Africa. Flies throughout the
year.

PRECIS OCTAVIA Cramer p 193
Gaudy Commodore

Identification Wingspan 4½–7cm. Species shows extreme seasonal dimorphism, the wet season form being pinkish-red, the dry season form blue chequered with black. ♂ pinkish-red with blackish-brown margins and spots; dry season form blue with black markings and a row of red submarginal spots. Intermediate specimens sometimes occur, more or less blue with a broad red band across both wings. Sexes similar.

Range and Habitat Open woodlands, savannah and bush country throughout the Ethiopian Region. Flies throughout the year, except in South Africa where it is on the wing from October to May.

Larval Food Plants *Coleus*, *Iboza*, *Pychnostachys* and *Plectranthus*.

PRECIS SOPHIA Fabricius p 193
Little Commodore

Identification Wingspan 3½–4cm. ♂ yellowish-brown with darker brown markings; sometimes median band white not yellowish. ♀ slightly larger with more rounded wings.

Range and Habitat A common forest species, occurring in forest glades and along roads and margins of forests, throughout most of the Ethiopian Region south to Malawi and Rhodesia. Flies near the ground. On the wing throughout the year.

PRECIS WESTERMANNI Westwood p 193
Blue-spot Commodore

Identification Wingspan 5½–6cm. ♂ black with a large orange-brown patch in each wing; round brilliant blue patch on anterior part of hindwing. ♀ pale orange-brown with dark brown markings.

Range and Habitat A common forest species in West Africa, the Congo, Uganda and Kenya. ♂♂ strongly attracted to animal droppings on roads. Flies throughout the year.

NYMPHALIDAE – NYMPHALIDS – DIADEMS

1 **HYPOLIMNAS MISIPPUS** ♂ ♀ ♀   *page* 180
   Compare ♀♀ with *Danaus chrysippus* (plate 9).

2 **HYPOLIMNAS MONTEIRONIS** ♂   182
   Sexes similar: no white spots on apex of forewing.

3 **HYPOLIMNAS ANTEVORTA** ♂   181
   Sexes similar: narrow blue band across hindwing.

4 **HYPOLIMNAS SALMACIS** ♂ ♀   182
   White spots in apex of forewing.

5 **HYPOLIMNAS DECEPTOR** ♂   184
   Sexes similar: inner margin of forewing black.

6 **HYPOLIMNAS DUBIUS** ♂ ♂   184
   Sexes similar: variable: some white on inner margin of forewing.

7 **HYPOLIMNAS MECHOWI** ♂   183
   Sexes similar: margin of pale hindwing patch dusky.

8 **HYPOLIMNAS DINARCHA** ♂ ♂   183
   Sexes similar: variable: hindwing patch ochreous.

9 **HYPOLIMNAS USAMBARA** ♂   185
   Sexes similar: orange-red patch on hindwing.

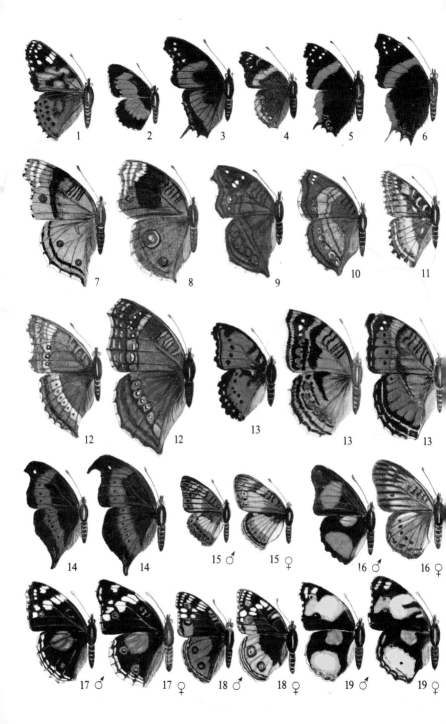

1   2   3   4   5   6

7   8   9   10   11

12   12   13   13   13

14   14   15 ♂   15 ♀   16 ♂   16 ♀

17 ♂   17 ♀   18 ♂   18 ♀   19 ♂   19 ♀

PLATE 22   193

NYMPHALIDAE – NYMPHALIDS

1 **VANESSA CARDUI** ♂   *page* 195
Sexes similar.
2 **VANESSULA MILCA** ♂   195
Sexes similar: broad orange-red band.
3 **ANTANARTIA DELIUS** ♂   196
Sexes similar: curved orange-brown forewing band.
4 **ANTANARTIA ABYSSINICA** ♂   195
Sexes similar: pale brownish-red bands: no tails.
5 **ANTANARTIA HIPPOMENE** ♂   196
Sexes similar: tail relatively short.
6 **ANTANARTIA SCHAENEIA** ♂   196
Sexes similar: tail relatively long.
7 **PRECIS TOUHILIMASA** ♂   188
Sexes similar: fore and hindwings deep blue.
8 **PRECIS ARTAXIA** ♂   188
Sexes similar: forewing mainly blue.
9 **PRECIS NATALICA** ♂   189
Sexes similar: reddish-brown markings with white spots on forewing.
10 **PRECIS TEREA** ♂   189
Sexes similar: curved brownish-yellow band.
11 **PRECIS CERYNE** ♂   190
Sexes similar: orange-brown and yellowish band.
12 **PRECIS ARCHESIA** ♂ ♂ seasonal forms   189
Sexes similar: row orange-brown hindwing spots.
13 **PRECIS OCTAVIA** ♂ ♂ ♂ seasonal forms   191
Sexes similar: distinct seasonal forms.
14 **PRECIS TUGELA** ♂ ♂   190
Sexes similar: orange-brown bands.
15 **PRECIS SOPHIA** ♂ ♀   191
Wing bands creamy-yellow or white.
16 **PRECIS WESTERMANNI** ♂ ♀   191
♂ blue spot on hindwing: ♀ reddish-brown with dark margin.
17 **PRECIS OENONE** ♂ ♀   194
Hindwing with round blue spot in ♂ and ♀.
18 **PRECIS ORITHYA** ♂ ♀   194
Hindwing mainly blue.
19 **PRECIS HIERTA** ♂ ♀   194
Hindwing with yellow patch and round blue spot.

PRECIS OENONE Linnaeus p 193
Blue Pansy

Identification Wingspan 4½–5½cm. ♂
forewing black with white spots; hindwing black with round blue patch in
centre of wing and small submarginal
eyespots. ♀ larger, usually with larger
eyespots on hindwing.
Range and Habitat An abundant
species in open woodland, savannah,
bush country and gardens throughout
the Ethiopian Region. Flies throughout the year.
Larval Food Plants *Asystasia*.

PRECIS HIERTA Fabricius p 193
Yellow Pansy

Identification Wingspan 4½–5½cm. ♂
blackish, large yellow patches on fore
and hindwings with heavy black markings; round blue patch in centre of
hindwing. ♀ larger with extra black
patch on yellow of forewing.
Range and Habitat An abundant
species in bush country, savannah,
open woodlands and gardens throughout the Ethiopian Region. Flies
throughout the year.
Larval Food Plants *Asystasia*, *Baleria*, *Justicia*, *Chaeloranthus* and *Ruellia*.

PRECIS ORITHYA Linnaeus p 193
Eyed Pansy

Identification Wingspan 4½–5½cm. ♂
forewing black with blue patch and
white markings; hindwing mainly deep
royal blue with black-ringed red eyespots. ♀ has larger eyespots.
Range and Habitat Abundant in open
dry country throughout the Ethiopian
Region. Flies throughout the year.
Larval Food Plants *Hygrophila*.

VANESSULA MILCA Hewitson
Orange and Brown

p 193

Identification Wingspan 4½–5cm. ♂ uniform dark brown with a broad orange median band across both wings. ♀ slightly larger.

Range and Habitat Forests of West Africa, the Congo to Uganda and western Kenya. Weak flier, often settling on foliage along forest paths and roads. Flies throughout the year.

♂ 3cm

VANESSA CARDUI Linnaeus
Painted Lady

p 193

Identification Wingspan 4½–7cm. ♂ orange to pinkish-brown; black apical patch spotted with white; heavy black spots on forewing; hindwing orange-brown with marginal and submarginal spots. ♀ similar.

Range and Habitat Abundant throughout the Ethiopian Region in a variety of open country habitats. Flies throughout the year.

♂

Larval Food Plants *Anchusa, Arctotis, Carduus, Echium, Filago, Lupinus, Madia, Malva, Urtica*, etc.

ANTANARTIA ABYSSINICA Felder
Ethiopian Admiral

p 193

Identification Wingspan 3½–4cm. ♂ the smallest of the African Admirals, blackish-brown with a slight golden tinge; dull orange-brown median band on forewing and white apical spots; orange-brown marginal band on hindwing; not tailed. ♀ similar.

Range and Habitat Edges of forest and wooded areas in highlands of Ethiopia, Kenya, northern Tanzania and eastern Uganda. Flies throughout the year.

Larval Food Plants *Urtica*.

♂

ANTANARTIA HIPPOMENE Hubner

p 193

Short-tailed Admiral

Identification Wingspan $4\frac{1}{2}$–$5\frac{1}{2}$cm. ♂♀ black, with red median band on forewing and white-spotted apical area; marginal band on hindwing; single short tail: underside variegated with green. The similar *Antanartia schaeneia* has a longer tail and underside marked with red-brown, not green.

Range and Habitat Mainly a forest and woodlands species found in West Africa, the Congo, Uganda, Kenya and Tanzania southwards to South Africa. Flies throughout the year except in extreme south where it is on the wing from September to April.

Larval Food Plants *Acalypha, Urtica.*

ANTANARTIA SCHAENEIA Trimen

p 193

Long-tailed Admiral

Identification Wingspan 5–6cm. ♂♀ black with red median band on forewing and white-spotted apical area; hindwing with marginal red band and a single long tail; anal angle sharply bifurcated; underside marked with red, not green.

Range and Habitat Usually highland forests and wooded areas in East Africa, south to eastern Rhodesia and South Africa. In the south of its range flies from October to April; throughout the year elsewhere.

Larval Food Plants *Boehmeria, Fleurya, Pouzolzia.*

ANTANARTIA DELIUS Drury

p 193

Orange Admiral

Identification Wingspan 5–6cm. ♂♀ blackish-brown with broad curved dark orange band on forewing, and row of subapical white spots; hindwing with broad dark orange band; black marginal band and tail. Curved forewing band and lack of red on margin of hindwing dis-

tinguishes this from related species.
Range and Habitat Forests and woodlands in West Africa and the Congo, east to Uganda, Kenya and Ethiopia, south to Tanzania. Flies throughout the year.
Larval Food Plants *Musanga.*

LACHNOPTERA AYRESII Trimen   p 176
Blotched Leopard
Identification Wingspan 5½–6½cm. ♂ orange-brown with dark brown markings; round grey scent scale patch on hindwing; hindwing sharply angled in centre of margin. ♀ larger and lacks the grey hindwing patch. The much paler and less heavily marked *Lachnoptera iole* of West Africa is probably conspecific.
Range and Habitat From the Congo, Uganda and Kenya south to South Africa. On the wing from October to April in South Africa; throughout the year further north.
Larval Food Plants *Rawsonia.*

PHALANTA COLUMBINA Cramer   p 176
Dusky Leopard
Identification Wingspan 5–6cm. ♂♀ dark orange-brown; relatively wide blackish submarginal markings; margin of hindwing angled near centre; underside with purplish-violet markings. The closely related *Phalanta phalantha* is orange-brown with a rounded hindwing.
Range and Habitat Mainly a forest or woodland species throughout the Ethiopian Region. Flies throughout the year.

PHALANTA PHALANTHA Drury

p 176

Common Leopard

Identification Wingspan 5–6cm. ♂♀ pale orange-brown with dark brown marginal and submarginal markings; hindwing margin rounded, not angled as in the closely related *Phalanta columbina.*

Range and Habitat A common species throughout the Ethiopian Region frequenting woodland, savannah and bush country. Flies throughout the year.

Larval Food Plants *Aberia, Doryalis,* and *Trimeria.*

ISSORIA HANNINGTONI Elwes

Hannington's Fritillary

Identification Wingspan 3½–4cm. ♂♀ pale orange-brown, merging to greenish at base; blackish-brown fore and hindwing margins with yellowish spots; line of round submarginal black spots on fore and hindwings and other blackish markings; underside hindwing chequered silver, red-brown and orange-yellow.

Range and Habitat Margins and glades of highland forests and marshy highland grasslands of Kenya. Flies throughout the year. Closely related species occur in western Uganda, the Cameroon Highlands, and mountains of southern Tanzania, Malawi, Zambia and eastern Rhodesia.

Larval Food Plants *Viola.*

FAMILY SATYRIDAE
BROWNS

This is a large family of sombre brown or greyish-brown butterflies, usually with rather short broad wings. Characters of the group include having the cells on both fore and hindwings closed; the main veins at the base of the forewing thick and swollen; palpi flattened with long bristly hairs. Flight slow and relatively weak, often near the ground. One genus – *Melanitis* – is largely crepuscular.

Early Stages. Many species lay their almost spherical eggs on various grasses. The larvae have forked tail segments: they may be smooth or covered with short hairs. The pupae are broad and often rounded, rarely angular.

MELANITIS LEDA Drury
Evening Brown

Identification Wingspan 6–7½cm. A large brown with a tailed hindwing; greyish-brown with an orange-brown apical patch on forewing enclosing a white-spotted black patch; orange-brown patch on hindwing. Sexes similar but dry season examples have longer tails. Underside patterned like a dead leaf.

Range and Habitat Common and widespread throughout the Ethiopian Region, inhabiting woodlands, forested areas, bush and plantations. Flies mainly at dusk, but may be disturbed during the day by walking through woodland undergrowth where it is resting. On the wing throughout the year.

Larval Food Plants Various grasses including *Setaria*, *Cynodon*.

GNOPHODES PARMENO Doubleday
Banded Evening Brown
Identification Wingspan 5½–6½cm. ♂♀
dark brown or greyish-brown with a
yellowish-buff apical band on forewing; hindwing tailed. Differs from
Melanitis leda in lacking the white-
spotted black forewing patch.
Range and Habitat Inhabits forests and
wooded areas throughout the Ethiop-

ian Region. Often flies towards dusk. On the wing throughout the year.
Larval Food Plants Various grasses.

AEROPETES TULBAGHIA Linnaeus
Mountain Beauty
Identification Wingspan 7–9cm. ♂
deep rich brown with rows of orange
spots across both wings: row of blue
submarginal eyespots on hindwing. ♀
larger and paler.
Range and Habitat High mountain
grasslands in South Africa, occurring
in Cape Province, Natal, Transvaal
and Orange Free State, north to Rhodesia. A rapid flier but attracted to

flowering plants. On the wing from December to April.
Larval Food Plants Various grasses including *Hebenstreitia, Hypparhenia* and
Stenotaphrum.

PARALETHE DENDROPHILUS Trimen
Bush Beauty
Identification Wingspan 4½–5½cm. ♂♀
orange-brown with blackish-brown
apical half of forewings spotted white
or yellowish; hindwing orange-brown
with blackish marginal band and dark
eyespots.
Range and Habitat Forested areas of
Eastern Cape, Natal and Northern

Transvaal, South Africa. Flies from November to April.
Larval Food Plants Various grasses.

BICYCLUS SAFITZA Hewitson
Common Bush Brown

Identification Wingspan 4–5cm. ♂ dark
brown with small apical patch tinged yellow;
two marginal white-centred black eyespots
on forewing; very small white spot near rear
margin of hindwing. ♀ paler and slightly
larger than ♂.

Range and Habitat An abundant and widely
distributed species throughout the Ethiopian
Region in wooded areas, gardens and forest
margins. Flies throughout the year. Many
other species of this genus have been described.

Larval Food Plants Various grasses.

YPTHIMA ASTEROPE Klug
African Ringlet

Identification Wingspan 3½–4cm. ♂♀ greyish-
brown with a pale apical patch on forewing
enclosing yellow-ringed white-centred eye-
spot; eyespot near rear margin of hindwing.
Faint eyespots on under surface. The dis-
tinctions between the various greyish-brown
Ypthima are difficult to detect, but in this
species the eyespots on the underside are not
very prominent.

Range and Habitat A common species
throughout the Ethiopian Region in wooded
areas, bush, savannah and grasslands. Flies
throughout the year.

Larval Food Plants Various grasses.

FAMILY LIBYTHEIDAE
SNOUTS

This is a very small family with a single common species in Africa. The Snouts are characterised by their angular shaped forewings and by the curious development of their palps. These are flattened and are four times as long as the head, projecting forwards like a snout. The forelegs are undeveloped in the ♂, well developed, with two claws, in the ♀. The African species is often highly gregarious, frequently encountered in swarms, sometimes migratory, settling on roads and mud.

Early Stages. The eggs are elliptical, bottle-shaped, and ribbed. The larvae are almost cylindrical, with fine hairs and two erect dorsal spines. The pupae are free-hanging, short like those of the family Nymphalidae.

LIBYTHEA LABDACA Westwood p 208
African Snout

Identification Wingspan 4–5cm. ♂♀ dark brown with angular forewings, paler and more rufous-brown in the southern and eastern race, *L. l. laius*; a subapical band of whitish spots on forewing and whitish or orange-buff markings. The species may be distinguished also by its very long forward-projecting palps.

Range and Habitat Common in forested and wooded areas throughout the Ethiopian Region, the race *L. l. laius* occurring in Tanzania south to Natal, South Africa. Often encountered in vast swarms which are more or less migratory. They settle in masses on roads and on damp mud or sand. Also readily attracted to, and settle on, perspiring human beings. Flies throughout the year.

♂

FAMILY RIODINIDAE
JUDYS

A small family, poorly represented in Africa but abundant in the tropics of Central and South America. The group is closely related to the Lycaenidae of which it is sometimes classified as a subfamily, but the forelegs of the ♂♂ are undeveloped and useless for walking; in the ♀♀ all six legs are developed. In the genus *Abisara* the hindwing is strongly angled or developed into a thick outward-angled tail. They are relatively weak fliers, and on settling hold their wings open.

Early Stages. Indian species related to those found in Africa lay their eggs singly on or near the food plant. The larva is thickset, tapering at each end, and is often covered with short hairs. The pupa is short and rather flattened; it is attached to the underside of a leaf at its anal end and supported by a silken girdle.

ABISARA DELICATA Lathy
African White Judy

Identification Wingspan 4–5cm. ♂♀ thick angled tail on hindwing; translucent white, slightly greyish at base; large brownish apical patch enclosing a white subapical band; two black and blue eyespots in yellowish patch on hindwing. Underside with larger subapical band.

4cm   ♂

Range and Habitat Local and uncommon in forested and wooded country in Kenya and Uganda, south to Malawi. Relatively weak flier. On the wing throughout the year.

ABISARA TALANTUS Aurivillius
Blue-patched Judy

p 208

Identification Wingspan 4–5cm. Hindwing sharply angled and elongated; ♂ forewing black with two blue bands, the lower of which extends along inner margin; two subapical eyespots; hindwing with blue and black eyespots on upper angle; costal margin bluish. ♀ brown with two whitish transverse bands followed by bluish band on forewing.

♂   4cm

Range and Habitat Forested areas of West Africa and the Congo. Flight relatively weak; occurs along forest paths. Flies throughout the year.

FAMILY LYCAENIDAE
BLUES

The Lycaenidae are a large and extremely complex group, numbering some 1050 species in Africa. With few exceptions this is a family of small or very small species. Many are of great beauty, having blue, violet or greenish sheens on the wings, and there are a number of brilliant coppery or red species, especially in South Africa. Many Lycaenids possess long tails, especially among the *Iolaus* and *Hypolycaena*. A few such as *Mimacraea* are mimics of Acraeas or Monarchs. Sexual dimorphism is frequent, and often the ♂ is more colourful than the ♀ and differently patterned. Characters of the group include having forelegs almost as well developed as the other two pairs; the forefeet of the ♂ usually unjointed and terminating in a single hook, whilst the ♀ has the forefeet jointed with two claws: antennae placed closely together. The Lycaenids vary greatly in their habits: some are weak, slow-flying insects, whilst others have an extremely rapid and strong flight. Some fly near the ground; others live high in forest trees.

Early Stages. Eggs usually spherical, flattened below, with pitting or ribbing. Larvae are short and broad with small heads. The pupae are thickset and rounded, free or attached to bark by a girdle.

MIMACRAEA MARSHALLI Trimen   p 208
Marshall's Acraea Mimic
Identification Wingspan 4½–5½cm. ♂♀ reddish-brown with or without a black apical patch; white subapical band. Resembles a miniature *Danaus chrysippus* and flies like that much larger and commoner species. Underside with round black spots at base of hindwing.

Range and Habitat Woodland and savannah country from Kenya south to Mozambique, Malawi, Zambia and Rhodesia. Has a buoyant, sailing flight, often settling on lichen-covered tree trunks.

Larval Food Plants Lichens.

♂   4cm

EPITOLA HEWITSONI Mabille p 208

Identification Wingspan 5–5½cm. ♂ bright blue with apical area and margins broadly black. ♀ blackish-brown with pale ochre-yellow sub-apical band and spot. Underside, forewing dark violet-brown; hindwing with black spots at base and in cell.

Range and Habitat Forest areas of Gabon and Portuguese Congo. On the wing throughout the year.

♂   4cm

EPITOLA POSTHUMUS Fabricius p 208

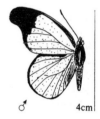

Identification Wingspan 6–7cm. ♂ brilliant metallic greenish-blue with black apical patch and narrow black marginal border. ♀ paler blue than in ♂ with wider black marginal band. Underside dark grey with metallic bronze-green apex and hindwing.

Range and Habitat Forest areas from West Africa to the Congo and western Uganda. Flies high, often settling on bare vines. On the wing throughout the year.

♂   4cm

AETHIOPANA HONORIUS Fabricius p 208

Identification Wingspan 4–6cm. ♂ bright blue with a large black apical patch enclosing blue spots; hindwing with narrow black border. ♀ forewing black with bluish-white discal band; hindwing bluish-white with broad black marginal band. Underside dark brown; subapical spots white; hindwing brownish-grey with black dots at base and white transverse line across centre.

Range and Habitat Forested areas of West Africa (Sierra Leone. Guinea, Cameroons and Gabon) to the Congo. Flies throughout the year.

♂   4cm

HEWITSONIA BOISDUVALI Hewitson   p 208

Identification Wingspan 5–6cm. ♂ forewing black with subapical band of bluish-white spots and blue patch near internal angle; hindwing black with large blue patch. ♀ differs in having the forewing subapical band and internal angle patch clear yellow. Underside, yellow on hindwing with black transverse stripes.

Range and Habitat Forested areas of West Africa from Guinea and Liberia through Ghana and Nigeria to Gabon and the Cameroons, eastwards to eastern Congo. Flies throughout the year.

♂   4cm

DEUDORIX ANTALUS Hopffer   p 208
Brown Playboy

Identification Wingspan 2½–3cm. ♂ pale bluish-brown with a slight coppery sheen; two black dots at anal angle of hindwing. ♀ paler and lacks slight coppery sheen. Underside greyish-white with dark brown transverse lines and spots. ♀ very similar to ♀ *Deudorix dinochares* but this species has red transverse lines on underside.

Range and Habitat A widespread and common species over most of the Ethiopian Region inhabiting savannah and bush country: often found on tops of small hills where there are bushes and trees. Flies throughout the year.

Larval Food Plants Larvae found in seed pods of *Crotolaria* and *Acacia*.

♂   4cm

DEUDORIX CAERULEA H. Druce   p 208
Blue Heart Playboy

Identification Wingspan 2½–3cm. ♂ bright pale blue with a dark blue patch on forewing; apical patch very pale brown. ♀ similar but lacks dark blue forewing patch and has pale brown marginal border to hindwing.

Range and Habitat Inhabits forest margins, woodland, savannah and bush country from tropical Africa south to Mozambique and northern South Africa. Flies throughout the year.

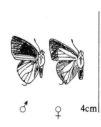

♂   ♀   4cm

DEUDORIX DINOCHARES Grose-Smith
p 208
Red Playboy

Identification Wingspan 2½–3cm. ♂ bright red with a dark brown apical patch. ♀ pale bluish-brown with a basal bluish patch on forewing; very similar to ♀ *Deudorix antalus* but distinguished by red lines and spots on underside.

Range and Habitat A common species over much of the Ethiopian Region, south to Natal and Transvaal, South Africa. Like its related species often found on bush-covered hilltops. Flies throughout the year.

♂ 4cm

Larval Food Plants Larvae found inside fruits of cowpea, peach and *Syzygium*.

DEUDORIX DIOCLES Hewitson
p 208
Orange-barred Playboy

Identification Wingspan 2½–3cm. ♂ forewing dark brown with a short red band; hindwing red. ♀ pale bluish-brown with a dark brown apical patch and costal band on forewing.

Range and Habitat A fairly common species in savannah and bush country from tropical Africa to South Africa. Habits similar to previous species, often found on summits of bush-covered hills. Flies throughout the year.

♂ 4cm

Larval Food Plants Pods of *Acacia*, *Crotolaria*, *Baphia* and *Bauhinia*.

MYRINA SILENUS Fabricius
p 208
Figtree Blue

Identification Wingspan 3–4cm. ♂ deep violet-blue with blackish-brown marginal borders and a red-brown subapical patch; long, thick tail. ♀ larger and with more extensive dark borders. The East and South African race, *Myrina silenus ficedula* is paler blue and the red-brown apical patch extends to margin of forewing.

Range and Habitat Widely distributed in Ethiopian Region to South Africa. Inhabits forested and wooded areas and savannah, where there are fig trees.

Larval Food Plants *Ficus*.

LIBYTHEIDAE, RIODINIDAE & LYCAENIDAE
SNOUTS, JUDYS & BLUES

1 **LIBYTHEA LABDACA LABDACA** ♂   *page* 202
   Sexes similar: long palps: dark brown.
2 **LIBYTHEA LABDACA LAIUS** ♂   202
   Sexes similar: long palps: rufous brown.
3 **ABISARA TALANTUS** ♂   203
   ♀ duller: hindwing strongly angled.
4 **MIMACRAEA MARSHALLI** ♂   204
   Sexes similar: apex of forewing either black or brown.
5 **EPITOLA HEWITSONI** ♂   205
   ♀ brown with ochreous subapical band on forewing.
6 **EPITOLA POSTHUMUS** ♂   205
   Sexes similar but ♀ paler.
7 **AETHIOPANA HONORIUS** ♂ ♀   205
   ♂ blue forewing spots: ♀ bluish-white forewing band.
8 **HEWITSONIA BOISDUVALI** ♂ ♂ u   206
   ♀ with yellow subapical band on forewing.
9 **DEUDORIX ANTALUS** ♂ ♀ u   206
   Sexes similar: underside greyish-white with dark brown transverse
   lines.
10 **DEUDORIX DINOCHARES** ♂ ♀ u   207
   ♀ underside with red transverse lines.
11 **DEUDORIX DIOCLES** ♂ ♀ u   207
   ♂ red forewing patch.
12 **MYRINA SILENUS FICEDULA** ♂ ♀ u   207
   Red-brown apical patch extends to margin forewing.
13 **MYRINA SILENUS SILENUS** ♂   207
   Sexes similar: black ringed apical patch.
14 **MYRINA DERMAPTERA** ♂ ♀ u   210
   No red-brown on forewing.
15 **HYPOLYCAENA PHILIPPUS** ♂ ♀ u   210
   Brown with slight mauve sheen.
16 **HYPOLYCAENA BUXTONI** ♂ ♀ u   210
   Underside whitish with fine transverse lines.
17 **IOLAUS COECULUS** ♂ ♀ u   211
   Underside forewing with five red bands.
18 **IOLAUS BOWKERI** ♂ ♀ u   211
   Upperside deep blue.
19 **IOLAUS MARMOREA** ♂ ♀ u   211
   Upperside pale bluish-white or white.

1   2   3   4   5

6   7 ♂   7 ♀   8 ♂   8 u

9 ♂   9 ♀   9 u   10 ♂   10 ♀   10 u

11 ♂   11 ♀   11 u   12 ♂   12 ♀   12 u   13

14 ♂   14 ♀   14 u   15 ♂   15 ♀   15 u

16 ♂   16 ♀   16 u   17 ♂   17 ♀   17 u

18 ♂   18 ♀   18 u   19 ♂   19 ♀   19 u

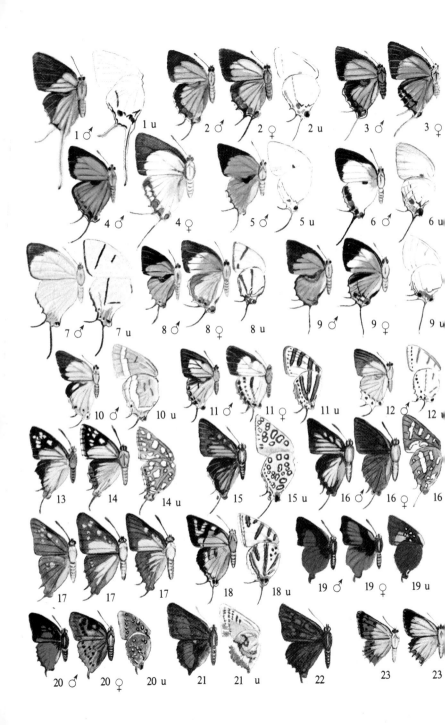

1 ♂ 1 u 2 ♂ 2 ♀ 2 u 3 ♂ 3 ♀

4 ♂ 4 ♀ 5 ♂ 5 u 6 ♂ 6 u

7 ♂ 7 u 8 ♂ 8 ♂ 8 u 9 ♂ 9 ♀ 9 u

10 ♂ 10 u 11 ♂ 11 ♀ 11 u 12 ♂ 12

13 14 14 u 15 15 u 16 ♂ 16 ♀ 16

17 17 17 18 18 u 19 ♂ 19 ♀ 19 u

20 ♂ 20 ♀ 20 u 21 21 u 22 23 23

PLATE 24   209

LYCAENIDAE – BLUES

1 **IOLAUS TIMON** ♂ u   *page* 212
   Sexes similar: very long
   thick tails.

2 **IOLAUS SILAS** ♂ ♀ u   212
   Prominent red spots on
   hindwing.

3 **IOLAUS CRAWSHAYI** ♂ ♀   213
   Smaller red spots on
   hindwing.

4 **IOLAUS LALOS** ♂ ♀   212
   ♂ no red spots on hindwing:
   ♀ bluish-white.

5 **IOLAUS MENAS** ♂ u   213
   ♀ white: underside white
   with thin black line on
   hindwing.

6 **IOLAUS ISMENIAS** ♂ u   213
   Sexes similar: two red spots
   on hindwing.

7 **IOLAUS PALLENE** ♂ u   214
   Sexes similar: pale yellow:
   heavy black lines on
   underside.

8 **IOLAUS SIDUS** ♂ ♀ u   214
   Underside, thick red band
   forewing, two on hindwing.

9 **IOLAUS SILANUS** ♂ ♀ u   215
   Three tails on hindwing.

10 **IOLAUS MIMOSAE** ♂ u   215
   Sexes similar: underside with
   white transverse band.

11 **IOLAUS APHNAEOIDES**
   ♂ ♀ u   215
   Thick orange or red bands on
   underside.

12 **IOLAUS AEMULUS** ♂ u   216
   Sexes similar: thin orange-
   red stripes on underside.

13 **APHNAEUS HUTCHINSONI**
   HUTCHINSONI ♂   *page* 217
   Sexes similar: wing margins
   black.

14 **APHNAEUS HUTCHINSONI**
   DRUCEI ♂ u   213
   Sexes similar: wing margins
   red-brown.

15 **APHNAEUS FLAVESCENS**
   ♂ u   217
   Sexes similar: silver-centred
   crimson rings on underside.

16 **APHNAEUS ORCAS** ♂ ♀ u   216
   Black-edged silver bands on
   underside.

17 **APHNAEUS ERIKSSONI**
   ♂ ♂ ♂   217
   Sexes similar: red-brown with
   or without blue patches.

18 **SPINDASIS NATALENSIS**
   ♂ u   218
   Sexes similar: V-shaped yellow
   bar forewing apex.

19 **AXIOCERSES AMANGA**
   ♂ ♀ u   218
   Pale streak at base of costa,
   forewing.

20 **AXIOCERSES**
   BAMBANA ♂ ♀ u   218
   No pale streak at base of
   costa, forewing.

21 **CAPYS ALPHAEUS** ♂ u   219
   Sexes similar: orange-brown
   patch on fore and hindwings.

22 **PHASIS THERO** ♂   220
   Sexes similar: orange-red
   spots on forewing.

23 **POECILMITIS THYSBE**
   ♂ ♂   221
   ♀ with rounder wings and
   restricted blue.

MYRINA DERMAPTERA Wallengren

p 208

Lesser Figtree Blue

Identification Wingspan 2½–3½cm. ♂ black with single thick tail; large blue patch on fore and hindwing. ♀ larger and with smaller blue patches. Underside mainly grey in both sexes. Differs from *Myrina silenus* in lacking red-brown apical patch on forewing.

Range and Habitat Occurs in savannah and bush country where there are fig trees, from East

Africa south to Natal and Eastern Cape Province, South Africa. Flies from October to April in the south, throughout the year further north.

Larval Food Plants *Ficus*, ? *Parinare*.

HYPOLYCAENA PHILIPPUS Fabricius

p 208

Purple Brown Hairstreak

Identification Wingspan 2½–3cm. ♂ pale brown with a distinct mauve sheen; hindwing with two black spots and orange and black spot in anal angle; below greyish-white with grey and orange lines. ♀ larger and paler, with double row of submarginal white spots. The closely related *Hypolycaena buxtoni* is paler on underside with thinner transverse lines.

Range and Habitat A common species in bush and savannah country through much of the Ethiopian Region. Settles on foliage of small trees and bushes. Flies throughout the year.

Larval Food Plants *Clerodendron*, *Ximenia*.

HYPOLYCAENA BUXTONI Hewitson

p 208

Buxton's Hairstreak

Identification Wingspan 2½–3cm. ♂ pale purplish-mauve, much brighter than ♂ *Hypolycaena philippus*; underside whitish with fine transverse lines. ♀ larger, with blackish border and apical patch.

Range and Habitat East Africa to South Africa (eastern Cape). Occurs in bush and savannah country and in open woodlands. Settles on foliage of trees and bushes. Flies throughout the year.

Larval Food Plants *Clerodendron*.

IOLAUS COECULUS Hopffer
p 208
Azure Hairstreak

Identification Wingspan 3½–4cm. ♂ bright violet-blue with black apical patch and margin to forewing. ♀ larger and paler with more extensive black marginal borders. Underside in both sexes greyish-white, with five red-brown bands on forewing and similar markings on hindwing.

Range and Habitat Occurs in bush and savannah country, woodland, margins of forests and

bush-covered hills in West Africa (Angola) and the Congo, eastwards to Tanzania, south to Natal and Transvaal, South Africa. Flies throughout the year.

IOLAUS BOWKERI Trimen
p 208
Bowker's Tailed Blue

Identification Wingspan 3½–4cm. ♂ bright pale blue with extensive black apical patch and white spots; underside whitish with brown lines and thick irregular bands. ♀ larger with more extensive spotting.

Range and Habitat Occurs in bush country, wooded areas and forest margins from northern Kenya, south to Cape Province. South Africa. Flies throughout the year, except in the south of its range where on the wing from October to April.

Larval Food Plants *Loranthus.*

IOLAUS MARMOREA Butler
p 208
Pale Tailed Blue

Identification Wingspan 3½–4cm. ♂ bluish-white with black apical patch and white spots: much paler than *Iolaus bowkeri* and with less white spotting; underside whitish with brown and grey markings. ♀ larger and whiter than ♂.

Range and Habitat Occurs in savannah and bush country in West Africa, eastwards across southern Sudan to north-western Uganda (West Madi) and western Kenya (Soy, Kitale and east

of Tororo). Flies throughout the year. Often attracted to flowering parasitic *Loranthus.*

Larval Food Plants *Loranthus.*

IOLAUS TIMON Fabricius
Congo Long-tailed Blue

p 209

Identification Wingspan $3\frac{1}{2}$–$4\frac{1}{2}$cm. ♂ easily recognised by its extremely long and relatively thick tails; apical half of forewing black, remainder powdery blue; hindwing blue with large black patch; underside whitish with orange and grey markings on hindwing. ♀ larger and usually paler.

Range and Habitat Forested and wooded areas, and bush at edge of forests, from West Africa and the Congo to Uganda. Usually flies high, settling on foliage of trees.

Larval Food Plants *Loranthus*.

IOLAUS SILAS Westwood
Sapphire Blue

p 209

Identification Wingspan $3\frac{1}{2}$–4cm. ♂ bright clear blue with black apical patch and black marginal border; two or three red spots on anal angle of hindwing; underside white with fine red line. ♀ larger, paler and often violet-blue; red submarginal band on hindwing. *Iolaus crawshayi* has less extensive red hindwing spots, but some examples are difficult to identify without examination of genitalia. *Iolaus lalos* ♂ lacks red spots, and ♀ mainly white, not blue.

Range and Habitat Bush and savannah country, coastal thickets and wooded areas in South Africa; it is also recorded from Rhodesia, Zambia, southern Congo and southern Tanzania and south-western Kenya. In South Africa on the wing mainly between October and May; flies throughout the year further north.

Larval Food Plants *Loranthus*.

IOLAUS LALOS H. Druce
Pale Sapphire Blue

p 209

Identification Wingspan $3\frac{1}{2}$–4cm. ♂ bright blue with black apical patch: distinguished from related species by absence of red spots on anal angle of hindwing; ♀ white, merging to violet-blue at base of wings; broad black apical patch on forewing.

Range and Habitat Inhabits coastal thickets,

bush and savannah country in coastal districts of Kenya, south to Tanzania, Malawi and Rhodesia. Flies throughout the year.
Larval Food Plants *Loranthus.*

IOLAUS CRAWSHAYI Butler

p 209

Crawshay's Sapphire Blue

Identification Wingspan 3½–4cm. ♂ bright blue with black apical patch and black marginal band; two or three small red spots on anal angle of hindwing; ♀ larger with larger red hindwing spots; forewing blue patch pale and often violet-blue. Very similar to *Iolaus silas* but red hindwing spots usually smaller.

♂ 4cm

Range and Habitat Open forest and wooded areas, bush country and coastal thickets and scrub in Kenya, Uganda, Tanzania, Ethiopia and Somalia. Flies throughout the year.
Larval Food Plants *Loranthus.*

IOLAUS MENAS H. Druce

p 209

Identification Wingspan 3½–4cm. ♂ brilliant blue with a black apical patch; underside white with a thin blackish line on hindwing. ♀ larger, white with a trace of blue towards base of fore and hindwings.

Range and Habitat Bush and savannah country and wooded areas in West Africa, Sudan, north-western Uganda, western Kenya and Tanzania where recorded from Tanga. Flies throughout the year.
Larval Food Plants *Loranthus.*

♂ 4cm

IOLAUS ISMENIAS Klug

p 209

Identification Wingspan 3½–4cm. ♂ white, merging to violet-blue at base of fore and hindwings; black apical patch and marginal bands; two red spots on anal angle of hindwing. ♀ similar but larger.

Range and Habitat Savannah and bush country, favouring bush and tree-covered hills, in West Africa, Sudan, Ethiopia and Uganda. Flies throughout the year.
Larval Food Plants ? *Loranthus.*

♂ 4cm

IOLAUS PALLENE Wallengren

p 209

Identification Wingspan 3½–4½cm. ♂ pale yellow with blackish apical patch and black marginal lines and tails; orange-red patch on anal angle of hindwing; underside with heavy black lines; ♀ larger and paler.

Range and Habitat Wooded and coastal bush and thickets in Kenya coastal districts, south to Mozambique, Rhodesia and northern Natal and Transvaal, South Africa. Flies throughout the year. Has some resemblance to a Pierid when flying.

Larval Food Plants *Loranthus*.

IOLAUS EURISUS Cramer

Identification Wingspan 3–3½cm. ♂ forewing black with a blue band along inner margin; hindwing blue with a black marginal line; underside creamy with reddish-brown transverse bands. ♀ paler, lavender-blue to clear blue at base.

Range and Habitat Forested and wooded areas, West Africa to the Congo. Flies throughout the year.

Larval Food Plants ? *Loranthus*.

IOLAUS SIDUS Trimen

p 209

Red Line Sapphire

Identification Wingspan 3–3½cm. ♂ bright blue with large black apical patch; hindwing blue without black margin; underside greyish with heavy reddish stripes. ♀ paler, often bluish-white on forewing.

Range and Habitat A common and wide-ranging species in bush and savannah country, woodlands and open forest in Kenya, southwards to Malawi, Rhodesia and South Africa. In South Africa on the wing from October to May; further north flies throughout the year. Often found on patches of parasitic *Loranthus* growing on trees.

Larval Food Plants *Loranthus*.

IOLAUS SILANUS Smith
p 209

Three-tailed Sapphire

Identification Wingspan 3–3½cm. Three tails; ♂ bright blue with large black apical patch on forewing and black marginal line on hindwing. underside white with hairlike dark lines and orange-red patch on anal angle of hindwing. ♀ larger with some white on forewing.

Range and Habitat Wooded and savannah country in eastern Kenya and north-eastern Tanzania: also recorded from the Congo.

Larval Food Plants *Loranthus.*

IOLAUS MIMOSAE Trimen
p 209

Identification Wingspan 3–3½cm. ♂ pale bright blue with black apical patch and black markings on hindwing; underside greyish with a whitish transverse band and narrow brownish lines. ♀ usually larger.

Range and Habitat Acacia woodland, bush and forest margins from Kenya south to South Africa. Flies throughout the year, except in extreme south of its range where it is on the wing from October/November to May.

Larval Food Plants *Loranthus.*

IOLAUS APHNAEOIDES Trimen
p 209

Identification Wingspan 3–3½cm. ♂ pale blue, often with whitish patch on forewing; black apical patch and black markings on hindwing; underside whitish with orange-brown or red-brown bands. ♀ paler, sometimes whitish, with more extensive black markings.

Range and Habitat Forested and wooded areas and thick bush from Kenya and Uganda south to South Africa. Flies throughout the year.

Larval Food Plants *Loranthus.*

IOLAUS ALIENUS Trimen

Identification Wingspan 3–3½cm. Forewings relatively long and outer margin concave: single tail. ♂ blue with black apical patch and black margins. ♀ larger and paler, and black markings more extensive.

Range and Habitat Bush and savannah country, often on bush-covered hills, in Uganda, Kenya and Tanzania, south to South Africa: also recorded from the Cameroons and northern Nigeria. West Africa. Flies throughout the year.

Larval Food Plants *Loranthus*.

♂   4cm

IOLAUS AEMULUS Trimen
Short-barred Sapphire

p 209

Identification Wingspan 3–3½cm. ♂ pale blue with a large black apical patch on forewing; underside white with reddish bands and row of black submarginal dots on fore and hindwings. ♀ similar but usually paler and larger.

Range and Habitat Inhabits bush and savannah country and woodland, from Kenya south to South Africa. On the wing from October to April in the south; flies throughout the year further north.

Larval Food Plants *Loranthus*.

♂   4cm

APHNAEUS ORCAS Drury

p 209

Identification Wingspan 2½–3cm. ♂ tailed, fore and hindwings blackish with large blue discal patch in both wings, divided by black veins. ♀ dark brown without blue markings. Underside brown or olive-brown with black-edged silvery bands: in eastern specimens edging red-brown.

Range and Habitat Forested and wooded areas in West Africa, the Congo, Uganda and western Kenya. These thickset blues are rapid fliers but often settle on regular perches: sometimes attracted to flowering bushes of the family Compositae. Flies throughout the year.

♂   4cm

APHNAEUS ERIKSSONI Trimen p 209
Eriksson's Highflier
Identification Wingspan 3–3½cm. ♂ tailed; a
robust reddish-brown species, with or without
pale blue basal patches; some dark-ringed
creamy spots usually present on forewing. ♀
resembles ♂ but is larger. Underside yellowish-
brown with silvery or orange spots.
Range and Habitat Inhabits bush country and
woodland, often found flying around bushes on
top of small hills. Ranges from Angola and
southern Congo through Rhodesia, Malawi and
Zambia to southern Tanzania. Flies throughout
the year.

APHNAEUS FLAVESCENS Stempffer p 209
Identification Wingspan 3–3½cm. ♂ tailed; black
with blue or greenish-blue markings on fore and
hindwings. ♀ similar but larger. Underside
creamy-yellow with crimson-ringed silvery
spots.
Range and Habitat A rare species known from
Malawi and from the Kenya coast in the Sokoke–
Arabuku forest. Flight rapid but settles frequently on foliage of trees; sometimes attracted
to flowering bushes. Flies mainly from January to May.

APHNAEUS HUTCHINSONI Trimen p 209
Hutchinson's Highflier
Identification Wingspan 3–4cm. ♂ tailed; bright
blue with white-spotted black apical patch on
forewing and a black border to hindwing. ♀
larger. Underside variable, yellowish to olive-
brown with large silver spots. The northern race,
A. h. drucei, has a red-brown marginal band on
fore and hindwings.
Range and Habitat Bush country, often found
flying around bushes on top of small hills, in

South Africa and Rhodesia. *A. h. drucei* occurs in Kenya, northern Uganda
and Tanzania. Specimens from Zanzibar are intermediate. In South Africa
flies from September to November: throughout the year further north.

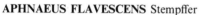

SPINDASIS NATALENSIS Doubleday & Hewitson   p 209
Natal Barred Blue

Identification Wingspan 2½–3cm. Sexes similar;
tailed; blue with a dark brown apical patch on
forewing containing a pale orange V. Underside
creamy-yellow with black-edged silvery or
rufous markings.

Range and Habitat Inhabits bush and wooded
country, often on small bush-covered hills, in
South Africa, Rhodesia and Mozambique. Flies
throughout the year, but most frequent from
October to March.

Larval Food Plants *Mundulea*, *Vigua*.

AXIOCERSES AMANGA Westwood   p 209
Bush Scarlet

Identification Wingspan 3–3½cm. ♂ forewing
blackish-brown with red streak at base of costa
and large triangular red patch on inner margin;
hindwing red with black base: tailed. ♀ paler,
more orange-red; red patch on forewing larger.
Underside reddish-brown with silver or whitish
streak at base of costa.

Range and Habitat Inhabits bush and savannah
country; often on bush-covered hillsides. Common in East Africa, south to
Transvaal and Natal, South Africa. Flies throughout the year.

Larval Food Plants *Ximenia*.

AXIOCERSES BAMBANA Grose-Smith   p 209
Scarlet

Identification Wingspan 3–3½cm. ♂ bright deep
red with black apical patch on forewing and
black costal stripe; hindwing red with variable
black border; tailed. ♀ orange-brown with
blackish border and markings on forewing and
black spots on hindwing. Underside pale red-
brown with silvery spots but without silvery
costal streak on forewing.

Range and Habitat A common bush, woodland and forest species in East
Africa south to South Africa. Flies throughout the year.

Larval Food Plants ? *Acacia*.

LEPTOMYRINA GORGIAS Stoll
Black Eye

Identification Wingspan 3–3½cm. ♂ pale brown with a bluish tinge; white-ringed black eyespots on lower margins of fore and hindwings; not tailed. ♀ usually larger with rounder forewings. Underside grey with irregular black lines.

Range and Habitat Occurs locally in bush country from the Cape, South Africa northwards to East Africa. In extreme south flies from September to April; on the wing throughout the year further north.

Larval Food Plants *Cotyledon*, *Crassula*, *Kalanchoe*, and *Mesembryanthemum*.

♂   4cm

LEPTOMYRINA HIRUNDO Wallengren
Tailed Black Eye

Identification Wingspan 2½–3cm. ♂♀ dark ashy-grey, paler and bluish towards base; long white tails; black spot at anal angle of hindwing. Underside white with fine orange-brown lines.

Range and Habitat Bush, wooded areas and margins of forest; usually flies low and is attracted to flowering succulents. Occurs in East, Central and South Africa. Flies throughout the year.

Larval Food Plants *Kalanchoe*, *Crassula*.

♂   4cm

CAPYS ALPHAEUS Cramer
Protea Scarlet

p 209

Identification Wingspan 3½–4½cm. ♂♀ dark brown with broad orange-red patch on fore and hindwings. Underside mainly pale grey with darker markings.

Range and Habitat Associated with *Protea* bushes; usually on rocky hillsides. Widespread in the Cape, South Africa, to Natal and northern Transvaal: local and uncommon in Rhodesia. Flies mainly in October, November and March.

Larval Food Plants *Protea*, the larva burrowing into the flower heads.

♂   4cm

PHASIS ARGYRASPIS Trimen
Warrior Copper

Identification Wingspan 3–4cm. ♂ bright orange-red with dark brown marginal bands and white-spotted fringe. ♀ usually larger with less angular wings. Underside, forewing mainly orange, hindwing pale brown with irregular silvery spots.

Range and Habitat Occurs on dry stony hillsides and rocky ground in the Cape and Orange Free

♂   4cm

State, South Africa. Attracted to flowering succulent plants. Flies from August to November, and from late February to April.

PHASIS THERO Linnaeus   p 209
Hooked Copper

Identification Wingspan 4–5½cm. ♂ dark rich brown with orange spots on forewing. ♀ larger. Underside, forewing with orange basal patch; hindwing grey with silvery hook-shaped markings in centre.

Range and Habitat Confined to Cape Province, South Africa, where it is widespread in coastal sandy areas and slopes of hills. Flies amongst bushes and small trees, often alighting on bare

♂   4cm

twigs. Flies mainly from September to November, with a second brood appearing in late March and April.

Larval Food Plants *Rhus, Melianthus.*

ALOEIDES MOLOMO Trimen
Molomo Copper

Identification Wingspan 2½–3cm. ♂♀ orange-brown with a broad dark brown marginal band on forewing, and a brown patch on costal margin; hindwing with a brown marginal patch followed by a thin dark marginal line. Underside, forewing pale orange-brown, hindwing vinaceous with black-edged pale spots.

Range and Habitat A local species found in the

♂   4cm

Cape, Transvaal and Orange Free State, South Africa, and in Rhodesia. Inhabits grassy hillsides and valleys: often settles on the ground. On the wing from September to March, commonest during October and November.

POECILMITIS CHRYSAOR Trimen
Golden Copper

Identification Wingspan 2½–3cm. ♂♀ brilliant reddish-copper with narrow black border to fore and hindwings; black dots on outer half of both wings: tailed. Underside pale orange-brown with a few dark brown and silvery dots; hindwing warm brown with a few indistinct markings.

♂   4cm

Range and Habitat Widespread but local in bush country and slopes of hills and mountains in Cape Province, Natal and Orange Free State, South Africa. Flies mainly during October–November, and during March.

Larval Food Plants *Rhus*, *Cotyledon* and *Zygophyllum*.

POECILMITIS THYSBE Linnaeus   p 209
Opal Copper

Identification Wingspan 2½–3cm. ♂ basal half to two-thirds of wings pale blue with metallic lustre; forewing apex bright orange-red with black margin; apical band of blackish spots; hindwing with orange-red to blackish margin. ♀ has rounder wings and basal blue patch smaller. Underside brown with silver or yellowish streaks and black dots. Species extremely variable.

♂   4cm

Range and Habitat Confined to South Africa where locally common from western Cape Province to the Drakensberg Mountains. Found in a variety of habitats from coastal dunes to bush-covered hillsides and mountain slopes. Flies from August to April.

Larval Food Plants *Aspalathus*, *Osteospermum*, *Zygophyllum*.

ANTHENE AMARAH Guerin
Black Striped Hairtail

Identification Wingspan 2½–3cm. The genus *Anthene* is characterised by having two (sometimes three) very short 'tails' on hindwing composed of tufts of hair. ♂ greyish-brown with golden sheen; black and orange dots at anal angle of hindwing. ♀ duller with more rounded forewing. Underside pale grey with black

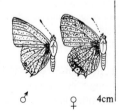

♂   ♀   4cm

dots and a black wedge near base of inner margin of forewing.
Range and Habitat A common species in bush country and wooded areas, often on flowering acacia bushes, throughout most of the Ethiopian Region. Flies throughout the year.
Larval Food Plants *Acacia* sp.

ANTHENE DEFINITA Butler
Common Hairtail

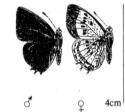

Identification Wingspan 2½–3cm. ♂ fore and hindwings deep purplish-blue without markings; very narrow black margins; three hair tufts. ♀ bluish-white, darker towards base, with broad brown marginal band and bands of dark spots. Underside pale grey with bands of elongated grey spots edged whitish.

♂   ♀   4cm

Range and Habitat A common species in eastern Africa, from Ethiopia southwards through Uganda and Kenya to South Africa. Frequents bush country, woodland and forest margins. Flies throughout the year.
Larval Food Plants *Acacia, Albizia, Bersama, Entada, Kalanchoe, Mangifera, Rhus.*

SYNTARUCUS TELICANUS Lang
Common Blue

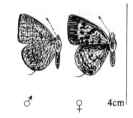

Identification Wingspan 2½–3cm. ♂ violet-blue with narrow black margin; hindwing with slender tail. ♀ blue at base to white with broad brown border and large black spots; hindwing with black marginal spots and other markings. Underside whitish with brown spots and lines.
Range and Habitat A common species ranging throughout the Ethiopian Region

♂   ♀   4cm

in bush country, savannah, woodland and gardens. Flies throughout the year.
Larval Food Plants *Burkea, Indigofera, Medicago, Melilotus, Plumbago.*

LAMPIDES BOETICUS Linnaeus
Long-tailed Blue
Identification Wingspan 2½–3½cm. ♂ violet-blue with a narrow brown border;

two small black spots at anal angle of hindwing; single slender tail. ♀ brown with strong bluish basal wash; marginal band of dark spots, edged white. Underside whitish with narrow brownish stripes; two orange and blue spots at anal angle of hindwing.

♂   4cm

Range and Habitat Common throughout the Ethiopian Region in a variety of habitats. Flies throughout the year.

Larval Food Plants The larvae feed on the seeds inside the seed-pods of *Crotolaria, Colutea, Dolichos, Indigofera, Lupinus, Medicago, Podalyria, Virgilia,* etc.

LYCAENA ORUS Cramer
Sorrel Copper

Identification Wingspan 2½–3cm. ♂♀ bright coppery-red with well-developed black margins; forewing with black dot in cell and row of submarginal black dots; tailless; slight violet lustre on the wings when viewed from certain angles. Underside, forewing orange-brown with pale brown margin; spotted black; hindwing pale brown without distinct markings.

♂   3cm

Range and Habitat A local species confined to South Africa, where it occurs in Cape Province, Natal, Transvaal and Orange Free State. Inhabits grasslands on mountain slopes, often in the vicinity of streams and marshes. Flies from October to March.

Larval Food Plants *Rumex.*

LYCAENA ABOTTII Holland
Abott's Copper

Identification Wingspan 2½–3cm. ♂ apex of forewing sharply angled; bright coppery-red with black margin and black spots on fore and hindwings. ♀ larger and forewing apex less acute; black spots usually heavier. Underside, forewing orange-brown with black spots; hindwing brown with indistinct, slightly reddish, marginal band and very indistinct greyish spots.

♂   4cm

Range and Habitat Highlands of Kenya and northern Tanzania in grassy places along margins of streams, marshes and edges of woodland. Flies throughout the year.

Larval Food Plants *Rumex.*

FAMILY HESPERIIDAE
SKIPPERS

The Skippers differ so greatly from other butterflies that some authorities consider they should have the status of a super-family, equal to that of all the other butterflies combined. Their wing structure is distinctive, the veins arising directly from the cells and not branching subsequently. The head is wider than the thorax and the eyes are large and protruding; the antennae are thickened towards the tip and are often hooked, and they are widely separated at the base. All six legs are well developed; the body is stout for the size of the insect.

With few exceptions the Skippers are relatively dull in colour, browns, greys and orange predominating. They have a characteristic rapid but erratic flight, tending to settle frequently. Some species rest with the wings closed above the back; others hold the wings half open with the hindwings dropped, whilst a few settle with the wings opened flat. Most are diurnal, being specially active during sunny periods, but a few species are crepuscular, flying mainly at dusk and dawn.

Early Stages. The eggs, usually laid singly on the food plant, may vary greatly in structure and their form is not indicative of the family. The larvae are cylindrical, tapering at both ends, but with large heads. They often live in a shelter of leaves which they spin together with silken threads in the manner of some moth larvae. The pupae are long and tapering, often enclosed in a loosely woven cocoon of silk and grass.

COELIADES FORESTAN Cramer
Striped Policeman
Identification Wingspan 5–5½cm. A large, robust species with hindwing

♂ ♂u

angled and elongated; forewing greyish brown, paler towards base; hindwing tinged orange at base and middle; anal angle fringed orange. Underside with broad white transverse band; no black spots. Sexes similar.

Range and Habitat A common species throughout the Ethiopian Region, found in bush country, wooded areas, savannah and forest margins. Settles with wings closed above back. Flies throughout the year.

Larval Food Plants *Combretum, Geranium, Solanum.*

TAGIADES FLESUS Fabricius
Clouded Flat

Identification Wingspan 4–5cm. ♂♀ brown with a greenish-grey wash on outer half of wings; forewing with transparent spots. Underside mainly white with dark costal border and black spots.

Range and Habitat A common species in wooded and forest areas throughout the Ethiopian Region. Flight fast and erratic but settles frequently on foliage with wings held open and flat. Flies throughout the year.

Larval Food Plants *Dioscorea.*

ABANTIS PARADISEA Butler
Paradise Skipper

Identification Wingspan 4–4½cm. ♂♀ forewing black or blackish-brown with numerous translucent white spots which are tinged yellow towards the base; hindwing with broad yellowish-white band, traversed by black veins; margin broadly black. Thorax with red spots; abdomen with red bands.

Range and Habitat Inhabits bush and rocky hills in eastern Africa from Somalia south to Tanzania, the southern Congo, Zambia, Malawi and Rhodesia to South Africa. Flies throughout the year.

Larval Food Plants *Cola, Hibiscus.*

ANDRONYMUS CAESAR Fabricius
White Dart

Identification Wingspan 4–4½cm. ♂♀ forewing
dark greyish-brown with a double band of translucent whitish spots; hindwing with a white
irregular patch. Underside, forewing greyish
with translucent spots; hindwing mainly white
with brown patch above anal angle and orange-
tinted marginal band.

Range and Habitat A locally common species
throughout most of the Ethiopian Region, in-
habiting wooded areas and forest. Flies throughout the year except in the
extreme south of its range.

♂   4cm

ARTITROPA ERINNYS Trimen
Bronze Spangled Skipper

Identification Wingspan 4½–5½cm. ♂♀ rich dark
brown; forewing with translucent angular spots
and an orange band across hindwing; fringe of
hindwing orange. Underside, blackish-brown
with translucent spotting on forewing; broad
white band across hindwing enclosing a single
round black spot.

Range and Habitat Occurs locally in East Africa,
south through Tanzania to Mozambique and
eastern Rhodesia to Natal, Transvaal and
eastern Cape, South Africa. Found in savannah
and wooded areas and in coastal bush. Flies
mainly at dusk and dawn. On the wing throughout the year, except in the
south.

Larval Food Plants *Dracaena*.

♂

BIBLIOGRAPHY

BERGER, L. A. (1950). Catalogues raisonnes de la Faune Entomologique du Congo belge. Lepidopteres–Rhopaloceres, 1. *Ann. Mus. Congo Belge,* Tervuren; Zool. (3) ii, 8.

BOORMAN, J. *and* ROCHE, P. (1957, 1965, 1959, 1961). The Nigerian Butterflies. Part 1 Papilionidae; Part 3 Euxanthe, Charaxes, Palla, Cymothoe; Part 5 Pseudacraea, Neptis, Kallima, Hypolimnas, Precis; Part 6 Acraeaidae. Ibadan University Press, Nigeria.

CARCASSON, R. H. (1960). The Swallowtail butterflies of East Africa. *J. E. Afr. nat. Hist. Soc.* Special supplement no. 6.

(1961). The Acraea butterflies of East Africa. *J. E. Afr. nat. Hist. Soc.* Special supplement no. 8.

(1963). The Milkweed butterflies of East Africa. *J. E. Afr. nat. Hist. Soc.* 24.

CARPENTER, G. D. H. (1935). The Rhopalocera of Abyssinia. *Trans. R. ent. Soc. Lond.* 83.

ELTRINGHAM, H. (1912). Monograph of the African species of the genus *Acraea. Trans. ent. Soc. Lond.*

(1922). On the African species of the genus *Neptis* Fab. *Trans. ent. Soc. Lond.*

EVANS, W. H. (1937). A catalogue of the African Hesperiidae in the British Museum. Brit. Mus. (nat. Hist.).

FOX, R. M., LINDSEY, A. W., CLENCH, H. K., *and* MILLER, L. D. (1965). The Butterflies of Liberia. *Mem. Amer. Ent. Soc.* 19.

GIFFORD, D. (1965). Butterflies of Malawi. The Society of Malawi (Historical and Scientific).

HERON, F. A. (1909). Ruwenzori Expedition reports: 12, Lepidoptera, Rhopalocera. *Trans. zool. Soc. Lond.* 19.

HOLLAND, W. J. (1920). Lepidoptera of the Congo. *Bull. Amer. Mus. nat. Hist.* 43.

MURRAY, D. P. (1936). South African Butterflies. A Monograph of the family Lycaenidae. London (John Bale).

PETERS, W. (1952). A Provisional Checklist of the Butterflies of the Ethiopian Region. Middlesex, England. (Classey.)

PINHEY, E. (1949). Butterflies of Rhodesia. Rhodesian Scientific Association, Salisbury.

(1965). The Butterflies of Southern Africa.

ROTHSCHILD, W. *with* JORDAN, K. (1898–1900). A Monograph of Charaxes and the allied Prionopterous Genera. *Novit. zool.* 5:7.

SEITZ, A. (1925). Macrolepidoptera of the world. v. 13 African Rhopalocera (by C. Aurivillius).

STEMPFFER, H. (1954). A revision of the genus *Aphnaeus* Hbn. *Trans. R. ent. Soc. Lond.* 105.

(1957). Les Lepidoptères de l'Afrique Noire Francaise. Fasc. 3. Lycaenides. *Init. afr., Dakar.* 14.

with BENNETT, N. H. (1958, 1959). Revision des genres appartenant au groups des *Iolaus* (Lycaenidae). 1, 2. *Bull. Inst. franc. Afr. Noire, Dakar.* 20, 21.

(1967). The Genera of the African Lycaenidae (Lepidoptera: Rhopalocera). *Bull. BM (NH) Ent.* Supplement 10.

SWANEPOEL, D. A. (1953). Butterflies of South Africa. Cape Town (Maskew Miller).

TALBOT, G. (1939). Revisional Notes on the genus *Colotis* Hubn. with a systematic list. *Trans. R. ent. Soc. Lond.* 88.

(1942). Notes on the genus *Colotis. Proc. R. ent. Soc. Lond.* (B) 11.

(1944). A preliminary revision of the genus *Mylothris. Trans. R. ent. Soc. Lond.* 94.

VAN SOMEREN, V. G. L. *with* ROGERS, K. st. A. (1925–1939). The Butterflies of Kenya and Uganda: Danaidae, Acraeinae, Nymphalinae (part). *J. E. Afr. nat. Hist. Soc.*

VAN SOMEREN, V. G. L. *with* JACKSON, T. H. E. (1952). The *Charaxes etheocles-ethalion* complex: a tentative reclassification of the group. *Trans. R. ent. Soc. Lond.* 103.

(1957). The *Charaxes etheocles-ethalion* complex: supplement no. 1. *Ann. Transv. Mus.,* Pretoria, 23.

VAN SOMEREN, V. G. L. (1963, 1964, 1966, 1967). Revisional notes on African Charaxes. Parts 1, 2, 3, 4. *Bull. BM (NH) Ent.* 13, 15, 18, 18.

VAN SON, G. (1949). The Butterflies of Southern Africa, Part 1. Papilionidae and Pieridae. Transvaal Museum Memoir No. 3.

(1955). The Butterflies of Southern Africa, Part 2. Nymphalidae, Danainae and Satyrinae. Transvaal Museum Memoir No. 8.

(1963). The Butterflies of Southern Africa. Part 3. Nymphalidae, Acraeinae. Transvaal Museum Memoir No. 14.

VILLIERS, A. (1957. Les Lepidoptères de l'Afrique Noire Francaise. Fasc. 2. Papilionides. *Bull. Inst. franc. Afr. Noire,* Dakar. 14.

INDEX

bohemani, **128**, 137
boueti, **112**, 130
brutus, **112**, 134
candiope, **97**, 127
castor, **113**, 133
catachrous, 155
cedreatus, 154, **160**
cithaeron, **128**, 138
cyhthia, **112**, 131
dilutus, **144**, 147
doubledayi, **160**, 163
druceanus, **113**, 135
epijasius, **113**, 132
etesipe, **145**, 148
ethalion, 153, **160**
etheocles, 153, **160**
eudoxus, **113**, 136
eupale, **144**, 146
fournierae, **143**, 144
fulgurata, 158
fulvescens, **97**, 126
gallagheri, 152
guderiana, 151, **160**
hadrianus, 142, **144**
hansali, **113**, 133
hildebrandti, **145**, 151
imperialis, 141, **144**
jahlusa, **129**, 147
jasius, **113**, 132
kahldeni, 143, **144**
lactitinctus, **112**, 131
laodice, **160**, 162
lasti, **112**, 130
lucretius, **112**, 131
manica, 157
mixtus, **129**, 139
mycerina, 162
nandina, **129**, 140
nobilis, 142, **144**
numenius, **128**, 137
opinatus, **145**, 150
paphianus, **145**, 148
pelias, **113**, 132
penricei, **145**, 149
phoebus, **113**, 135
pleione, **145**, 147
pollux, **112**, 134
porthos, 159, **160**
protoclea, **112**, 127
pythodorus, **129**, 142
saturnus, **113**, 132

thysi, **145**, 151
tiridates, **129**, 138
usambarae, 158
varanes, **97**, 125
viola, 156, **160**
violetta, **128**, 136
virilis, 155, **160**
xiphares, **129**, 140
zelica, **160**, 162
zingha, **144**, 148
zoolina, **144**, 146
Chief, 104
Clouded Flat, 225
Clouded Yellow, African, **65**, 95
Coeliades forestan, 224
Colias electo, **65**, 95
Colotis agoye, **81**, 92
    antevippe, **81**, 90
    aurigineus, **80**, 85
    calais, **80**, 85
    celimene, **80**, 86
    danae, **80**, 90
    elgonensis, **80**, 89
    eris, **81**, 93
    erone, **80**, 87
    eucharis, **81**, 90
    euippe, **81**, 91
    eunoma, **80**, 88
    evagore, **81**, 92
    evenina, **81**, 91
    halimede, **80**, 87
    hetaera, **80**, 88
    hildebrandti, **80**, 89
    ione, **80**, 87
    pallene, **81**, 92
    protomedia, **81**, 86
    regina, **80**, 88
    subfasciatus, **81**, 93
    vesta, **80**, 86
Commander, Naval, 188, **193**
Commodore, 188, **193**
    Blue-spot, 191, **193**
    Brown, 189, **193**
    Eared, 190, **193**
    Gaudy, 191, **193**
    Little, 191, **193**
    Marsh, 190, **193**
    Soldier, 189, **193**
Copper, Abott's, 223
    Golden, 221

Hooked, **209**, 220
Molomo, 220
Opal, **209**, 221
Sorrel, 223
Warrior, 220
Crenidomimas concordia, 167
Crimson Tip, **80**, 88
　Elgon, **80**, 89
　Three Spot, **80**, 88
Cymothoe, Blood Red, **161**, 167
Cymothoe beckeri, **161**, 166
　egesta, **161**, 166
　lurida, **161**, 166
　sangaris, **161**, 167
　theobene, **161**, 165
Cynandra opis, 170, **176**
Cyrestis camillus, 174, **176**

Danaid, Ansorge's, 102
　Dusky, 103
Danaidae, 100
Danaus chrysippus, **96**, 100
　formosa, **96**, 101
　limniace, **96**, 101
Deudorix antalus, 206, **208**
　caerulea, 206
　dinochares, 207, **208**
　diocles, 207, **208**
Diadem, 180, **192**
　Black-tipped, 182, **192**
　Blue, 182, **192**
　Blue Banded, 181, **192**
　Deceptive, 184, **192**
　Mechow's, 183, **192**
　Usambara, 185, **192**
　Variable, 184, **192**
Dixeia doxo, 79
　pigea, 78
　spilleri, 78
Dotted Border, **65**, 79
　Dusky, **65**, 83
　False, **65**, 77
　Swamp, 83
　Trimen's, 79
　Tropical, 82
　Twin, **65**, 82
　Yule's, 82

Epitola hewitsoni, 205, **208**
　posthumus, 205, **208**
Eronia cleodora, **65**, 93
　leda, **65**, 94

Euphaedra eleus, **161**, 169
　neophron, **161**, 168
　ruspina, **161**, 169
　spatiosa, **161**, 168
Eurema brigitta, **65**, 98
　desjardinsi, **65**, 99
　hapale, **65**, 99
　hecabe, **65**, 98
Eurytela dryope, **177**, 178
　hiarbas, **177**, 178
Euxanthe crossleyi, **97**, 125
　eurinome, **97**, 125
　tiberius, **97**, 124
　trajanus, **97**, 123
　wakefieldi, **97**, 124

False Acraea, Trimen's, 172, **176**
False Diadem, 173, **176**
False Fritillary, 170, **176**
False Wanderer, 172, **176**
Forester, Gold Banded, **161**, 168
　Orange, **161**, 169
Forest Queen, **97**, 124
Friar, **96**, 102
Fritillary, Hannington's, 198

Gnophodes parmeno, 200
Golden Tip, **80**, 89
　Banded, **81**, 93
Graphium adamastor, 66
　agamedes, 63
　almansor, 62
　atheus, **64**, 71
　auriger, 61
　aurivilliusi, 63
　colonna, **64**, 68
　fulleri, 62
　gudenusi, **64**, 68
　hachei, 60
　illyris, **64**, 67
　junodi, **64**, 70
　kirbyi, **64**, 67
　latreillianus, 59, **64**
　leonidas, **64**, 66
　morania, 57
　nigrescens, **64**, 69
　odin, 62
　olbrechtsi, 63
　philonoe, **64**, 66
　policenes, **64**, 70
　polistratus, **64**, 69

porthaon, **64**, 71
pylades, 58
ridleyanus, 58, **64**
simoni, **45**, 61
taboranus, 58
tynderaeus, 59, **64**
ucalegon, 60, **64**
ucalegonides, 61
weberi, 60
Grass Yellow, Angled, **65**, 99
  Broad-bordered, **65**, 98
  Common, **65**, 98
  Pale, **65**, 99.
Guineafowl, 169, **176**

Hairstreak, Azure, **208**, 211
  Buxton's, **208**, 210
  Purple Brown, **208**, 210
Hairtail, Black Striped, 221
  Common, 222
Hamanumida daedalus, 169, **176**
Hesperiidae, 224
Hewitsonia boisduvali, 206, **208**
Highflier, Eriksson's, **209**, 217
  Hutchinson's, **209**, 217
Hypolimnas antevorta, 181, **192**
  deceptor, 184, **192**
  dinarcha, 183, **192**
  dubius, 184, **192**
  mechowi, 180, **192**
  misippus, 180, **192**
  monteironis, 182, **192**
  salmacis, 182, **192**
  usambara, 185, **192**
Hypolycaena buxtoni, **208**, 210
  philippus, **208**, 210

Inspector, Garden, 189, **193**
Iolaus aemulus, **209**, 216
  alienus, **209**, 216
  aphnaeoides, **209**, 215
  bowkeri, **208**, 211
  coeculus, **208**, 211
  crawshayi, **209**, 213
  eurisus, **209**, 214
  ismenias, **209**, 213
  lalos, **209**, 212
  marmorea, **208**, 211
  menas, **209**, 213
  mimosae, **209**, 215
  pallene, **209**, 214

sidus, **209**, 214
silanus, **209**, 215
silas, **209**, 212
timon, **209**, 212
Issoria hanningtoni, 198

Joker, **161**, 175
  Common, **161**, 178
Judy, African White, 203
  Blue-patched, 203, **208**
Judys, 203

Kallima ansorgei, **177**, 180
  cymodoce, **177**, 180
  jacksoni, **177**, 179
  rumia, **177**, 179

Lachnoptera ayresii, **176**, 197
Lampides boeticus, 222
Layman, **96**, 104
Leaf Butterfly, African, **177**, 179
  Ansorge's, **177**, 180
  Jackson's, **177**, 179
  Western, **177**, 180
Lemon Traveller, **81**, 93
Leopard, Blotched, **176**, 197
  Common, **176**, 198
  Dusky, **176**, 197
Leptomyrina gorgias, 219
  hirundo, 219
Leptosa alcesta, 84
  medusa, 83
Libythea labdaca, 202, **208**
Libytheidae, 202
Lilac Beauty, **177**, 187
Lilac Tip, **80**, 86
Lycaena abottii, 223
  orus, 223
Lycaenidae, 204

Map Butterfly, African, 174, **176**
Melanitis leda, 199
Migrant, African, **81**, 98
Mimacraea marshalli, 204, **208**
Monarch, African, **96**, 100
  Beautiful, **96**, 101
  Blue, **96**, 101
Monarchs, 100
Monk, 102
Mother of Pearl, **177**, 186
  Clouded, **177**, 187

Mylothris bernice, 83
  chloris, **65**, 79
  poppea, **65**, 82
  rhodope, 82
  sagala, **65**, 83
  trimenia, 79
  yulei, 82
Myrina dermaptera, **208**, 210
  silenus, 207, **208**

Nepheronia argia, **65**, 95
  thalassina, **65**, 94
Neptis saclava, 173
Nymphalidae, 123
Nymphalids, 123
Novice, **96**, 103
Nymph, Blue Banded, 170, **176**
  Brown Tree, 175
  Forest Glade, 170, **176**
  Lilac, 174, **176**
  Obscure Tree, 175
  Speckled Lilac, 167
  Velvety, 174

Orange and Brown, **193**, 195
Orange and Lemon, **65**, 94
Orange, Double-banded, **80**, 85
  Veined, **80**, 86
Orange Tip, African, **81**, 91
  Bushvelt, **81**, 92
  Small, **81**, 92
  Smoky, **81**, 91
  Sulphur, **81**, 90
Painted Empress, **177**, 179
Painted Lady, **193**, 195
Palla decius, **161**, 164
  publius, 164
  ussheri, **161**, 164
  violinitens, 165
Pansy, Blue, **193**, 194
  Eyed, **193**, 194
  Yellow, **193**, 194
Papilio aethiops, 43
  andronicus, 53
  antimachus, 33, **36**
  bromius, **44**, 46
  charopus, **36**, 43
  constantinus, **37**, 38
  cynorta, **45**, 53
  dardanus, 35, **36**
  demodocus, **44**, 50

  echerioides, **45**, 54
  euphranor, 41
  fulleborni, 55
  gallienus, **45**, 51
  hesperus, **37**, 40
  hornimanni, **36**, 42
  jacksoni, **45**, 55
  leucotaenia, **37**, 48
  lormieri, **44**, 49
  mackinnoni, **37**, 42
  magdae, **44**, 47
  mechowi, **45**, 51
  mechowianus, **45**, 52
  menestheus, **44**, 49
  nireus, **44**, 48
  nobilis, **37**, 39
  ophidicephalus, **44**, 50
  pelodorus, 40
  phorcas, **37**, 38
  plagiatus, 54
  rex, 34, **36**
  sjostedti, 56
  sosia, **44**, 47
  thuraui, **37**, 46
  zalmoxis, 34, **36**
  zenobia, **45**, 52
  zenobius, 52
  zoroastres, **45**, 57
Papilionidae, 33
Paralethe dendrophilus, 200
Pardopsis punctatissima, 122
Phalanta columbina, **176**, 197
  phalantha, **176**, 198
Phasis argyraspis, 220
  thero, **209**, 220
Pieridae, 72
Pinacopteryx eriphia, **80**, 84
Piper, Golden, **177**, 178
  Pied, **177**, 178
Pirate, **177**, 188
Playboy, Blue Heart, 206
  Brown, 206, **208**
  Orange-barred, 207, **208**
  Red, 207, **208**
Poecilmitis chrysaor, 221
  thysbe, **209**, 221
Polka Dot, 122
Pontia helice, 84
Precis archesia, 189, **193**
  artaxia, 188, **193**
  ceryne, 190, **193**

hierta, **193**, 194
natalica, 189, **193**
octavia, 191, **193**
oenone, **193**, 194
orithya, **193**, 194
sophia, 191, **193**
terea, 189, **193**
touhilimasa, 188, **193**
tugela, 190, **193**
westermanni, 191, **193**
Pseudacraea boisduvali, 172, **176**
eurytus, 172, **176**
lucretia, 173, **176**
poggei, 172, **176**
semire, 171, **176**
Pseudargynnis hegemone, 170, **176**
Pseudoneptis coenobita, 171, **176**
Pseudopontia paradoxa, 72
Purple Tip, **80**, 87
    Coast, **80**, 87
    Regal, **80**, 88

Red Tip, **81**, 90
Ringlet, African, 201
Riodinidae, 203

Sailer, Small Spotted, 173
Salamis, Blue, **177**, 185
    Blue-banded, **177**, 186
Salamis anacardii, **177**, 187
    cacta, **177**, 187
    cytora, **177**, 186
    parhassus, **177**, 186
    temora, **177**, 185
Sapphire, Red Line, **209**, 214
    Three-tailed, **209**, 215
Satyridae, 199
Scarlet, **209**, 218
    Bush, **209**, 218
    Protea, **209**, 219
Scarlet Tip, **80**, 90
Skipper, Bronze Spangled, 226
    Paradise, 225
Skippers, 224
Snout, African, 202, **208**
Snouts, 202
Spindasis natalensis, **209**, 218
Striped Policeman, 224
Sulphur Tip, Speckled, **81**, 92
Swallowtail, Abyssinian Blue-banded, 43

Acraea, 58, **64**
African Giant, 33, **36**
Angola White Lady, 58
Black and Yellow, 37, 40
Blue-spotted Black, **37**, 46
Broad Blue-banded, **44**, 46
Bush Kite, 41
Citrus, **44**, 50
Constantine's, **37**, 38
Coppery, 59, **64**
Cream-banded, **37**, 48
Drury's Emperor, **44**, 49
Eastern Black and Yellow, 40
Emperor, **44**, 50
Fulleborn's, 55
Fuller's, 62
Giant Blue, 34, **36**
Godman's, **44**, 47
Green-patch, **37**, 38
Green-spotted, 59, **64**
Horniman's, **36**, 42
Jackson's, **45**, 55
Kilimanjaro, 56
Mackinnon's, **37**, 42
Mechow's, **45**, 51
Mocker, 35, **36**
Narrow Blue-banded, **44**, 48
Noble, **37**, 39
Regal, 34, **36**
Simon's, **45**, 61
Straight-banded, **44**, 47
Tabora, 58
Veined, **64**, 66
Weber's, 60
Western Emperor, **44**, 49
Westwood's, **36**, 43
White-banded, **45**, 54
White-dappled, **64**, 66
White Lady, 57
Swallowtails, 33
Swordtail, Cream-striped, **64**, 71
    Dancing, **64**, 69
    Dusky, **64**, 69
    Kigezi, **64**, 68
    Kirby's, **64**, 67
    Large Striped, **64**, 71
    Mamba, **64**, 68
    Mozambique, **64**, 70
    Small Striped, **64**, 70
    Yellow-banded, **64**, 67
Syntarucus telicanus, 222

Tagiades flesus, 225

Vagrant, Cambridge, **65**, 94
  Large, **65**, 95
  Vine Leaf, **65**, 93
Vanessa cardui, **193**, 195
Vanessula milca, **193**, 195

Wanderer, **96**, 107
White, African Common, 75
  African Small, 79
  African Veined, 75
  African Wood, 84
  Anthill, 78
  Brown-veined, 76
  Congo, 73

Congo Wood, 83
Diverse, 74
Forest, 76
Last's, 73
Meadow, 84
Moth-like, 72
Orange-patch, **80**, 87
Raffray's, **64**, 76
White Dart, 226
Woodland, 73
Zebra, **80**, 84
Whites, 72

Yellow, Spiller's, 78
  Veined, **81**, 86
Ypthima asterope, 201